SUNSHINE KITCHEN

VANESSA BOLOSIER

SUNSHINE KITCHEN

DELICIOUS CREOLE RECIPES FROM THE HEART OF THE CARIBBEAN

PAVILION

TO PAPA, WHOSE HEART
AND SOUL WILL LIVE FOR
EVER IN MY KITCHEN.

CONTENTS

INTRODUCTION: WELCOME TO MY CREOLE KITCHEN

In *Creole Kitchen*, you'll find sunshine and laughter, childhood memories, ancestral stories and recipes that blend traditions and the culinary skills of everyone I've learned from throughout the years.

Over centuries, the Caribbean islands where I grew up – Guadeloupe and Martinique – have seen many changes and cultural influences; my food celebrates, honours and remembers those influences, but also innovates, develops and adapts. My Creole kitchen is a rich hybrid, resulting from the meeting of four continents. It reflects the Amerindians' love of seafood, the African tradition of using tubers in slow-cooked stews, French, Spanish, Portuguese, Dutch and English cooking techniques applied to tropical ingredients, and Asia's myriad of spices, used whenever possible. In my Creole kitchen, you will encounter aromas you've never smelled before; for me, these smells remind me of home and trigger an instant sense of comfort.

I want this book to bring people together around the thing that matters the most when you celebrate life on the islands: food. It includes some treasured memories, such as the first time I was allowed to make a meat stew for Sunday lunch, thereby joining my family's 'good cook club'. It also looks at the traditions and festivals that give Creole cuisine its tempo. For instance, Christmas food was planned months ahead by fattening the pig for at least six months and drying orange peel to make the sacrosanct 'shrubb' rum punch.

Most of all, the food and drinks from my Creole kitchen are easy to make, easy to enjoy, easy to share. The recipes are based on classic dishes from Guadeloupe and Martinique; I have given them my personal touch and you can adapt them to your taste. We are lucky to be living at a time when it is increasingly easy to find tropical vegetables and fruit in supermarkets, Asian and Afro-Caribbean shops and markets, but in some recipes I have also suggested alternative ingredients to enable you to make them wherever you are.

I hope that these recipes will bring your friends and family together in the same way they have mine throughout the years. They will transport you to a tropical paradise and warm your heart and soul – or better still, inspire you to visit the islands of the French Caribbean. My *Creole Kitchen* is for the curious and the adventurous cook, with delicious recipes from my kitchen to yours.

WHAT IS CREOLE?

When you say the word Creole, many people automatically think of New Orleans, Louisiana. But Louisiana represents only a very small part of Creole culture. Creole was born of the convergence of many different peoples and cultures. They needed fto communicate, and from that necessity arose a common language, albeit with a huge variety of dialects and accents, and a culture that embraces music and dance, art and architecture, folklore, myths, literature, games, rituals, festivals and, above all, food.

The English word 'creole', the French 'créole', Spanish 'criollo' and Portuguese 'crioulo' all derive from the verb 'criar' ('to breed') and the Latin 'creare' ('to create'). It is associated with people who were born in a former colony – as opposed to those who migrated there as adults. My definition of Creole people, with regards to the Caribbean – one that many people in the region will agree with – is that they are the descendants of slaves and labourers from different parts of Africa and Asia, living together on islands colonized by the French and English.

Creole people are mainly found in Haiti, Guadeloupe, Martinique, Dominica, French Guiana and Saint Lucia, and also in Louisiana, Mauritius, the Seychelles and Réunion islands. Other islands, such as Grenada, Saint Thomas and Trinidad, have a residual Creole culture.

I'm a Creole from the French Caribbean, so most of my focus is specifically on Guadeloupe and Martinique, where my parents were born. Guadeloupe and Martinique are overseas regions as well as départements of France, as are French Guiana in South America and Réunion in the Indian Ocean. All these places are French governed, with French as the official language; the inhabitants are born French nationals, they study the French curriculum in schools and vote in all the French elections. They are part of the European Union – scattered pieces of France between the Atlantic and Caribbean Sea.

Map of the Lesser Antilles, showing Guadeloupe and Martinique.

CREOLE FOOD: THE MELTING POT

Creole food is one of the first fusion foods, drawing influences from trading and cultural mixing since the 16th century. It reflects the rich diversity of the environment in which it developed – the land, the ocean, the climate – and also the diversity of people on the islands. All these elements created a vibrant cuisine. And although some might see the history of my island developing through slavery as a cause of sorrow, I embrace it and find in it tremendous wealth.

I would have to say that my African ancestors have had the greatest impact on my personal identity. However, I can't ignore the influence my Amerindian great-grandmother had on my father, who passed on his knowledge of food and cooking to me. I also can't ignore my European roots – the result of a romance between a French pirate and an Amerindian he met and settled down with after he stopped off in Marie-Galante. Creole cuisine is full of stories of that sort, with the richness that comes from the intermingling of the islands' many settlers.

AMERINDIANS

The first settlers on the islands now known as the Petites Antilles (Lesser Antilles) were the Arawak, who arrived from South America in around 100BC. After the ninth century, the Arawak were conquered by another South American people, the Kalinas or Kalinago, better known as the Caribs. The Amerindians were hunters, fishermen and farmers.

The early food culture was based on what was available on each island. The Amerindians of the Lesser Antilles were known as 'people of the sour cassava civilization'. They cleared land on which to grow cassava and maize. Cassava (also known as manioc or yucca) is a starchy tuberous root, which can be boiled and eaten or ground to make flour. The flour was primarily used to make *kassav*, a flatbread cooked on a large round skillet heated over a wood fire, or *boucan*. With the juice of sour cassava, they made *ignari*, a sauce with hot chilli peppers. They also made a fermented cassava drink called *ouicou*.

The indigenous Caribbeans lived near rivers and on the coast. Crabs, conch, prawns (shrimp), crayfish, lobster, fish (such as grouper, tuna, snapper and shark), whale, dolphin and tortoises were the staples of their diets. They also hunted various birds, rabbits and other animals. In terms of cooking techniques, the Amerindians invented the barbecue: they grilled food on a framework of sticks, called *barbacoa*.

Native plants included *piments* (chilli peppers), *ananas* (pineapple), *pomme cannelle* (sweetsop or sugar apple), *corossol* (soursop), guavas and coconuts. Cassava (manioc), sweet potato, pumpkin and certain types of peas and beans also grew wild on the islands.

EUROPEANS

When Columbus came back to the Americas for the second time in 1493, the first island he set foot on was Kalouacera (or Karukera) – which means 'the island of beautiful waters' – the name given by the Kalinago Amerindians to my native island, Guadeloupe. Columbus renamed the island 'Santa Maria de Guadalupe', to fulfil a promise made during a pilgrimage in Spain at the convent of Santa Maria de Guadalupe de Extremadura. Explorers and colonizers renamed the islands and waterways, calling the region the West Indies because Columbus was hoping he was close to India and its abundance of spices.

The Spanish introduced foods such as onions, garlic, coriander (cilantro), chickpeas and oranges. Other Europeans, including the Portuguese, Dutch, Danish, British, French and Swedish, came later to the islands, bringing their culinary trademarks such as the use of saltfish (from Portugal), pickling techniques and various cakes and sweets. They also introduced foods from their trade with Asia, such as rice, limes, ginger, mangoes and *malaka* (malacca apple, plum rose or pomerac). Vanilla, native to Central America, was introduced to the Antilles by the French. Breadfruit was introduced from Tahiti in the late 18th century as a cheap source of high-energy food for slaves. The breeding of domesticated animals such as pigs, cows and chickens replaced hunting as a source of meat.

Generally, the meals cooked for the colonizers were not eaten by anyone else. Most Creole cooking is a legacy of the slaves and indentured servants and when it came to meat, as they were left the parts of the animals that the Europeans didn't want, it is why pigs' tails, cow's feet, tripe and other offal are frequently found in Creole single-pot stews.

However, a number of dishes brought during colonization were fully integrated into Creole cuisine: beef patties are a twist on British Cornish pasties; black pudding (*boudin noir*, blood sausage) was enjoyed in many parts of Europe, as were baked goods such as tarts, bread and desserts, such as rice puddings.

AFRICANS

The Caribbean was colonized by Europeans for the cultivation of commodities such as sugar cane and bananas. However, the locals did not take kindly to the idea of being reduced to slave labour on their own land. Around 60 years of conflict resulted in the partial extermination of the Amerindians (through fighting, alcohol and exposure to new diseases) and the colonizers had to seek another labour force: they found it in West Africa.

Most African slaves were abducted to produce sugar, molasses, rum and bananas, which had become very important foods in the Caribbean. I take pride in the fact that my African ancestors made these crops highly profitable, despite the hot, strenuous and dangerous conditions of the plantations. If they hadn't been forced into labour, they would have enriched the African continent, it's true, but as a descendant I can now take credit for the wealth of many western countries, which was built on the profitability of this trade. I embrace the history that makes me who I am and the slave trade was part of it.

In Africa, the diet would have included cassava and cornmeal, yams, dasheen (taro), ground-nuts (peanuts/monkey nuts), watermelon, okra, pigeon peas, plantains and bananas. These were transported to the New World along with the slaves – and their goats for milk and meat.

Although slow-cooked food is a direct heritage from the African continent, it was reinforced by the lifestyle of slaves on the plantations. Slow-cooked stews would simmer throughout the day as they worked long hours and, furthermore, vegetables such as cassava and dasheen are toxic unless thoroughly cooked, while offal, such as tails and feet, needs a long cooking time to become tender.

If fish or vegetables were available, the slaves would use them in quick-fried foods such as fritters (*accras*) made with cornmeal. (Wheat flour entered the diet later, and is what's mainly used nowadays for fritters and other fried foods.)

On some plantations, subsistence farming was common. The slaves grew plants from their native land, and crossed native and foreign species. If they grew more than they needed, the slave women would sell it in the Sunday markets, a practice that exists to this day in Guadeloupe and Martinique – and pretty much throughout the Caribbean.

ASIANS

After slavery was abolished in 1848, plantation owners still needed low-cost labour to continue running their profitable trade. Immigrants from India arrived in the Caribbean, bringing their own ingredients like mango and aubergine (eggplant), distinctive cooking styles and spices. After they served their years pf indentured servitude, many Indians decided to make a go of it on their own and built a small community of farmers. Their descendants still own melon, pineapple and vegetable plantations. They also farm the best goats to make Colombo curry (now considered one of the 'national dishes' of the French Caribbean).

WHAT'S IN MY CREOLE KITCHEN

There are a few basic utensils and ingredients you will need to recreate the atmosphere of a Creole kitchen and cook Creole food.

POTS AND UTENSILS

First among these is an old-school, very large, cast-iron pot with a tight-fitting lid, known in the United States as a Dutch oven. Creole food is family-style cooking so it's about quantity. A large, heavy-duty aluminium pot with a lid is an alternative found in many Caribbean kitchens. Lids are very important. I don't encourage you to cook Creole food in non-stick pans; sometimes you need the food to stick to create good flavours at the bottom of the pan, which you then deglaze with water, lime juice or vinegar.

Other utensils are mostly things you may already have in your kitchen:
• large bowls for marinating
• some good sharp knives
• slotted spoons
• a wooden spatula or two
• a colander
• a sharp grater with large, medium and small holes, for grating coconuts, lime zest and spices such as nutmeg and cinnamon.
• I use my food processor to save hours of chopping and grinding.
• I also use a juicer to make coconut milk and pineapple juice.

For Creole cooks, the '*kwi*' is a kitchen essential. It's half an emptied and dried calabash gourd, used as a cup, bowl, scoop or container for fresh spices, onions, garlic, limes and chillies. My grandmother has one, my mother has one and I have one. It's a thing you see in every Creole kitchen.

For making drinks and syrups, you will need some empty rum bottles (have a *ti' punch* party and keep the bottles) and a funnel. If you're using recently emptied rum bottles, there's no need to sterilize them – the lingering rum aromas will add a touch of extra character. Otherwise you will need to sterilize them. Wash your bottles in hot water with antibacterial washing up liquid, place them in a preheated oven 110°C/225°F/gas mark ¼ for 15 minutes and then remove them using oven mitts. You can use the same method for a metal funnel but if you have a plastic funnel just wash it in hot water with antibacterial liquid.

INGREDIENTS

- Vegetable oil
- Sunflower oil
- White vinegar
- Coconut vinegar – not essential, but we use it in many recipes in the same way as simple white vinegar, for example to deglaze a cooking pan
- Maggi (also known as KubOr) cubes – exported around the world for more than a hundred years, we often use these as a seasoning, crumbled into sauces and stews

Spices
- Allspice – a berry (known locally as *bois d'inde*) that combines the flavours of cloves, nutmeg and cinnamon. We use it in many savoury dishes and it's easy to find ground allspice in shops and supermarkets.
- Black pepper
- Cinnamon – for a good fresh cinnamon flavour I use a cinnamon stick and grate it just before I need it. 'A pinch' of cinnamon would be equal to giving the stick four strokes over the small holes of your grater.
- Cloves
- Colombo powder (p.86)
- Fresh ginger
- Mixed spice – a blend of ground cinnamon, nutmeg, ginger and cloves (sometimes including allspice), similar to the pumpkin pie spice sold in the United States. I often use it with meat.
- Nutmeg – always use freshly grated nutmeg; a whole nutmeg will keep for ages in an airtight container. For 'a pinch' of grated nutmeg, stroke it four times over the small holes of your grater.
- Vanilla (preferably fresh vanilla pods, otherwise use vanilla extract)

Herbs
- Bay leaves
- Garlic
- Parsley
- Fresh thyme – very important

Fruits and vegetables
- Avocados – large green ones
- Breadfruit – canned are fine when not in season
- Chillies – we use mainly hot varieties such as bird's-eye, habanero and Scotch bonnet
- Coconuts – some recipes call for grated fresh coconut meat and unsweetened desiccated (dry) coconut can often be substituted; canned coconut milk is usually an acceptable substitute for fresh
- Mangoes
- Onions
- Pineapples – keep a few cans of pineapple slices in the cupboard
- Spring onions – we use both the white and the green parts
- Tomatoes

Beans and peas (most types are available in both dried and canned forms)
- Mixed peas and beans
- Brown lentils
- Green pigeon peas (gungo peas) – frozen, dried or canned
- Red kidney beans

DRINKS

Guadeloupe and Martinique are among the most prolific rum-producing islands, producing some of the world's best rum — *rhum agricole* — which is distilled from fresh sugar cane juice rather than molasses. On Sundays, my dad would take the whole family on long drives to explore the island and he often told us stories about the illustrious past of Guadeloupe in the sugar and rum trade. As I write, I can recall the smell of molasses from the factories we drove past and visited.

I love all rums, but I wouldn't have my cocktails made with anything other than *rhum agricole*, since, just like Obelix, I fell into this magic potion at an early age. However, there are some very good industrial rums that can replace *rhum agricole*; the cocktail will not taste quite the same but will still be delicious.

Some of these drinks need to macerate or mature for a few weeks or months. You'll need some sterilized glass jars or empty rum bottles and a funnel to pour the liquid into the containers.

COCONUT PUNCH

Having *punch coco* for Christmas in the Caribbean Creole islands is a tradition, like having eggnog in the USA or mulled wine in the UK. From the time I was eight years old, and my brother was five, we were allowed a finger of coconut punch every Christmas, which we loved not for the rum, but for its deliciously creamy taste.

Serves 8–10

200ml/7fl oz/scant 1 cup white rhum agricole
400ml/14fl oz/1⅔ cups coconut milk
200g/7oz/scant 1 cup condensed milk
150ml/5fl oz/⅔ cup cane syrup (p.198)
2 pinches grated cinnamon
1 pinch grated nutmeg
grated zest of 1 lime
1 vanilla pod, cut in half lengthwise

Put the rum, coconut milk, condensed milk and cane syrup in a large mixing bowl. Stir with a wooden spoon until rich and thick.

Add the cinnamon, nutmeg and lime zest. Using a small knife, scrape the seeds from the vanilla pod and add to the bowl. Stir until evenly mixed.

Using a funnel, pour the coconut punch into an empty rum bottle (sterilized if necessary, see p.22) and place in the refrigerator for at least 2 hours. You can keep it in the refrigerator for up to 2 months.

Shake well before serving.

TIP

This is best made with freshly grated cinnamon stick and whole nutmeg, and a fresh vanilla pod. However, you can use ground cinnamon and nutmeg, and replace the vanilla pod with 1 tablespoon vanilla extract.

LICCI

I have always loved lychees. This fruit is very rare in Guadeloupe and mainly grows on the leeward coast. If you're lucky enough to know someone who has a tree to give you a box or two every season, you make the most of it.

Serves 4

500ml/18fl oz/2 cups cane syrup (p.198)
juice of 8 limes
125ml/4fl oz/½ cup white *rhum agricole*
125ml/4fl oz/½ cup coconut water
4–8 lychees, peeled and deseeded – use canned lychees if not in season
crushed ice

Pour the cane syrup into a jug. Add the lime juice, rum and coconut water and stir until thoroughly mixed. Place in the refrigerator for at least 3–4 hours.

Put some crushed ice into each glass and add one or two lychees, then pour in the cocktail.

PEANUT PUNCH

While some settled for coconut punch, my father always took it one step further: peanuts, cocoa – he made punch out of everything! I can't get enough of this.

Serves 8

250g/9oz monkey nuts, shelled
1 can (about 400g/14oz) condensed milk
1 can (about 400g/14oz) evaporated milk
3 pinches grated cinnamon
2 pinches grated nutmeg
½ vanilla pod, split lengthwise
1 bottle (70cl) white *rhum agricole*

Put the peanuts, condensed milk, evaporated milk, cinnamon and nutmeg in a food processor. Using a small knife, scrape the seeds from the vanilla pod into the mixture, then blend to a smooth paste.

Transfer the paste to a mixing bowl and add the rum. Stir to mix. Using a funnel, pour the punch into the empty rum bottle. Close the bottle and leave the punch in a cupboard away from any light for a week.

Shake well before serving with an ice cube.

PAPACOCO

When you have papaya trees, you know they can be very prolific. In the Caribbean, a *bavaroise* has come to mean a milky (and often alcoholic) fruit drink – quite different from the creamy, fruity French dessert *bavarois* that is set with gelatine. The most popular *bavaroises* are soursop, papaya and guava. When my dad used to make this milky drink with papaya juice after our morning run on Sundays, I knew we were in for a treat even though papaya wasn't my favourite thing. He made it with condensed milk, but here I've used rum and coconut milk and made it an adult drink.

Serves 4

2 large ripe papayas, peeled, halved, seeds scooped out
600ml/20fl oz/2½ cups coconut milk
400ml/14fl oz/1⅔ cups white *rhum agricole*
1 pinch grated cinnamon
1 tsp vanilla extract

Blend the papaya flesh with the coconut milk, then pass through a sieve into a bowl.

Add the rum, cinnamon and vanilla and stir.

Transfer to a cocktail shaker and shake well, or pour into a large jug and whisk vigorously. Put some ice cubes into each glass and pour in the cocktail. Drink immediately, before the papaya starts to separate from the milk.

SHRUBB

Shrubb is a very traditional Christmas liqueur – the drink my dad loved to make above all others. My father's childhood wasn't the best – he grew up very poor and Christmas held a very precious place in his heart because it was the only time of year he was really allowed to be a child, have fun and indulge. Dad would have stars in his eyes when talking about this drink, and from October we would eat mountains of oranges so he could dry the peel to make shrubb. He made several types: strong shrubbs, sweeter ones, a mild version for the children and flavoured shrubbs with star anise in some, cardamom in others, or a mix of orange and clementines. His shrubbs infused for a good 40 days to be perfect and ready to be downed during Christmas celebrations.

Makes about 1.2 litres/
2 pints/5 cups

3 oranges
1 bottle (70cl) white *rhum agricole*
500ml/18fl oz/2 cups cane syrup
   (p.198)
1 cinnamon stick
1 pinch grated nutmeg
1 star anise
1 vanilla pod, cut in half lengthwise

Peel the oranges in long strips, keeping only the skin (zest) and ensuring that none of the white flesh is left on. Leave to dry for at least a week, preferably in direct sunlight.

Once dry, place the orange peel in the bottle of rum and leave to infuse for a week.

Pour the rum and orange peel into a sterilized 1.5 litre/2½ pint/1.5 quart preserving jar. Add the syrup, cinnamon, nutmeg, star anise and vanilla pod and mix well. Leave to infuse for 3 weeks.

Strain the rum through a fine sieve into a large jug, discard the peel and spices and pour back into the empty rum bottle, using a funnel. It will keep in a dark cupboard for 6 months.

Serve with an ice cube.

TIP

Back home, we buy rum in 1.5 litre bottles, one of which would be ideal for this recipe. If you haven't got one of these, use two smaller bottles and/or a 1.5 litre preserving jar.

TI' PUNCH

Ti' punch is simply a Creole institution, a real representation of the culture of Guadeloupe and Martinique. *Ti' punch* is a very easy to make short cocktail and tradition demands that it is not prepared in advance: instead, the ingredients are left on the table for each guest to make up their own. Almost like a ritual, you have to take your time, sip and savour.

This cocktail can only be made with rhum agricole; it can be white or aged, but don't you dare try to make a *ti' punch* with anything else. It would be a sin, just as adding an ice cube would be considered a real insult to the purists. Don't underestimate this little punch. Drink it moderately.

This is the basic recipe for one person, but make it your own, that's what *ti' punch* is all about.

Serves 1

½ lime
2 tsp golden caster sugar
    or light soft brown sugar
    (or 1 tsp cane syrup, p.154)
50ml/2fl oz/generous 3 tbsp *rhum agricole*

Squeeze the lime into a small glass (keep the squeezed lime) and add the sugar.

Stir with a teaspoon (or, if you have one, a *bwa lélé*, a small stick with branches at the end, used as a whisk) until the sugar has dissolved.

Put the squeezed lime in the glass. Pour in the rum (no ice). Enjoy!

SORREL (HIBISCUS) DRINK

When people are enjoying their rum-laced sorrel punch during the extended Christmas celebrations called *Chanté Nwèl*, this sorrel drink is the non-alcoholic alternative. It's a festive, spicy drink, reminiscent of my childhood singing carols in Creole throughout Advent and Christmas.

Serves 4

100g/3½oz dried sorrel (hibiscus)
   petals
1 cinnamon stick
1 litre/1¾ pints/4 cups water
30g/1oz granulated raw cane sugar
1 tbsp vanilla sugar
 a few mint leaves (optional)

Put the sorrel, cinnamon and water in a saucepan. Bring to the boil and boil for 15 minutes, then leave to cool.

Scoop out the petals. Add the brown sugar and vanilla sugar and stir well until the sugar has dissolved. Place in the refrigerator for at least 3 hours.

Serve with ice, and a few mint leaves if you like.

TIP

In the Caribbean, sorrel means the red flower of the hibiscus. We use it to make drinks (both alcoholic and non-alcoholic) and in cakes. You may be more familiar with it than you think: it's used in herbal teas for its colour and flavour. You can buy dried hibiscus flowers in Afro-Caribbean, Turkish and Persian shops.

GINGER JUICE

This recipe isn't technically completely Creole. My West African boyfriend craved his favourite childhood drink, and so his mother taught me how to make this juice. One day during a trip back home, I served it to my mother and cousins. They argued that this drink was the soft version of a well-known love cocktail reputed to ignite amorous flames, which includes a so-called aphrodisiac bark we call *bois bandé*. Not sure how true that is, but this juice will definitely give you a kick when needed.

Serves 4

100g/3½oz fresh ginger, peeled
300g/10½oz pineapple, peeled, or 300g/10½oz drained canned unsweetened pineapple slices or chunks
juice of 3 limes
1 litre/1¾ pints/4 cups water
350g/12oz/1¾ cups golden granulated sugar

Process the ginger and pineapple in a juicer. Transfer to a bowl or large jug, add the lime juice and stir, then add the water and stir well until thoroughly mixed. Alternatively, if you don't have a juicer, blend the ginger and pineapple with the lime juice and water and then pour through a sieve.

Add the sugar to the juice and stir well until the sugar has dissolved. Place in the refrigerator for at least 3 hours.

Serve with ice cubes.

TIP

To transform this cocktail into a love potion, add some rum and grated cinnamon.

PASSION FRUIT PUNCH

This punch is the type of drink you are offered when visiting elderly people. When I used to stay with my grandfather in Marie-Galante or my godmother in the countryside, we often visited older neighbours. Grandmas would open a kitchen cupboard and reveal large bottles of punches like this one. Some of them would have been there for years. My cousins and I would serve it to those sitting around the table playing dominoes or cards. Purists drink it without ice, but when I was old enough to have it, an ice cube mellowed it for me.

Serves 10

6 passion fruits
150g/5½oz/¾ cup golden
   granulated sugar
1 vanilla pod, cut in half lengthwise
1 bottle (70cl) white *rhum agricole*
1 cinnamon stick

Cut the passion fruits in half and scoop out the pulp into a large mixing bowl. Add the sugar, vanilla pod and rum and stir to mix.

Using a funnel, pour the punch into the empty rum bottle. Insert the cinnamon stick into the bottle. Close the bottle and leave the punch to mature for at least 6 weeks in a cupboard. It will keep for up to 6 months.

Serve in a short glass with two ice cubes.

PLANTEUR

Planteur is as much a tradition as *ti' punch* (p.24) in the Caribbean. I was taught from an early age that planteur is the ladylike cocktail to order. It's my mother's favourite. Always on the menu in any local restaurant, it's very mellow and is traditionally based on the principal of balancing various fruit juices with rums of different ages. Angostura bitters is an alcoholic mixer flavoured with infused spices and herbs. It's a relatively recent addition, dating back to the 1970s, when the French islands increased their trading links with the rest of the Caribbean. This is my take on planteur.

Serves 6–8

175ml/6fl oz/¾ cup mango juice
225ml/8fl oz/scant 1 cup pineapple
   juice
200ml/7fl oz/scant 1 cup guava
   juice
2 tbsp white *rhum agricole*
3 tbsp aged *rhum agricole*
zest of 2 limes, peeled in strips, and
   juice of ½ lime
1½ tsp Angostura bitters
   (approximately 40 drops)
3 tbsp cane syrup (p.154)
1 cinnamon stick
1 pinch grated nutmeg
3 tbsp grenadine syrup (p.158)

Put all the fruit juices, rums, lime juice, Angostura bitters and cane syrup into a large bowl. Stir to mix, then pour into a large jug or two. Add the cinnamon stick, nutmeg and lime zest. Place in the refrigerator for 2 hours.

To serve, pour a little grenadine syrup into each glass. Pour in the cocktail and add an ice cube.

TIP

You can decorate the cocktail
with finely sliced fresh fruits
such as mango or pineapple.

STARTERS

◆ ◆ ◆ ◆ ◆ ◆ ◆ ◆ ◆

Creole culture is all about community, and it's perfectly natural for relatives, friends or neighbours to turn up on your doorstep at any time. Chances are they'll end up in the kitchen, with you whipping up some of these dishes to share. Out comes the *ti' punch*, accompanied by fritters of all sorts (or whatever you have in your refrigerator or cupboard). When you sit down to a big family dinner, you will find not one but four or five of these starters combined in an *assiette creole* (Creole platter). They tend to be light and delicious to pique your appetite for the heavy stuff coming as mains.

If you have a deep-fat fryer for making fritters, awesome. If not, be extremely cautious with the oil. It should be hot but, if it starts to smoke, it means it's too hot and the outside of your fritters will burn while the inside won't be cooked. Don't fry with oil that smokes.

AVOCADO FÉROCE (MARTINIQUE)

Traditionally eaten by workers in the cane and banana fields of Martinique, they would start the day with it as a filling breakfast, often accompanied by what they called *décollage* or 'white coffee' – a small glass of white rum. In recent years this dish has taken a starring role in the *didiko* (Creole brunch).

Serves 4

300g/10½oz skinless, boneless dried salted cod
1 lime, halved
2 large ripe green avocados
200g/7oz coarse cassava flour (gari)
¼ onion, very finely chopped
2 garlic cloves, crushed and very finely chopped
⅓ Scotch bonnet chilli, deseeded and very finely chopped
1 sprig parsley, very finely chopped
salt and freshly ground black pepper

Preheat the oven to its hottest setting: 250°C/480°F/gas mark 9 or 10.

Put the saltfish in a saucepan, add cold water to cover, bring to the boil and boil for 5 minutes. Drain the water.

Put the fish in an ovenproof dish and cook in the oven for 5 minutes. Remove from the oven, cover with cold water and leave to soak for about 5 minutes.

Drain the water and pat the fish dry with paper towels. Put the fish in the food processor and blend to a fine purée. Squeeze the juice of half a lime over it.

Peel the avocados, chop them into small pieces and mash them with a fork or potato masher until smooth. Add the cassava flour and mix to a thick paste. Add the fish, onion, garlic, chilli and parsley. Squeeze the other half of the lime over the mixture, then season to taste. Form small balls and serve immediately.

TIP

Gari is a coarse cassava flour sold in Afro-Caribbean shops. If you can't find it, replace with 200g/7oz rough oatcakes, blended in the food processor.

DRESSED CRAB

This is an essential element in any *assiette creole* (Creole platter). Blue land crab is now a protected species in the French Caribbean and it is only hunted at specific times of the year, but when the hunting season is open there are countless ways of cooking it. For this recipe, you can boil sea crabs with bay leaves and salt, then pull out the flesh from the claws and legs; you will also need to wash and sterilize the shell before filling it. To save time, I suggest you buy crabmeat from the fishmonger.

Serves 4

70g/2½oz baguette (quarter of a baguette), slightly stale is best
3 tbsp semi-skimmed (lowfat) milk
2 spring onions (scallions)
1 onion
3 garlic cloves
2 sprigs parsley
1 sprig thyme, leaves only
½ red habanero (or Scotch bonnet) chilli, deseeded
4 tbsp butter
175g/6oz crabmeat, shredded
juice of 1 lime
salt and freshly ground black pepper
3 tbsp fresh or dried breadcrumbs

Preheat the oven to 180°C/350°F/gas mark 4. Soak the baguette in the milk for 10 minutes.

Put the spring onions, onion, garlic, parsley, thyme and chilli in a food processor and blend until very finely chopped.

Melt 2 tablespoons of the butter in a frying pan (skillet). Add the chopped onion mixture and cook for a minute. Add the crabmeat and lime juice and cook for 2 minutes. Remove from the heat.

Squeeze the milk out of the bread. Put the bread in the food processor and blend to a purée. Add the bread purée to the crab. Put the pan over a medium heat and cook for 3–4 minutes, stirring regularly so it doesn't stick to the pan. Season with salt and pepper to taste. Remove from the heat.

Place the stuffing in small ramekins (if you used a whole crab, fill the cleaned shell with the stuffing) and sprinkle the breadcrumbs over. Top each ramekin with ½ tablespoon of butter. Place in the oven for 10 minutes. Serve hot.

Suggestion: Serve the crab on its own with salad, or as part of a Creole platter with saltfish fritters (p.42) and fish boudins (p.46).

SALTFISH CHIQUETAILLE

A classic Creole starter. *Chiquetaille* **means 'shred'. My mother always gets angry with me when she desalts her saltfish and I come into the kitchen to steal large pieces of not-yet-desalted cod and just munch away – I can't resist it. We serve this with cucumber salad and one or two slices of avocado. But sometimes we have it in a baguette for a morning snack or in a** *bokit* **(see p.100) for dinner.**

Serves 4

600g/1lb 5oz skinless, boneless dried salted cod
2 tbsp sunflower oil
1 onion, very finely chopped
3 spring onions (scallions), very finely chopped
3 garlic cloves, crushed and very finely chopped
½ red habanero chilli, deseeded, very finely chopped
2 sprigs parsley, very finely chopped
1 sprig thyme, leaves only
2 tomatoes, very finely chopped
1 lime

Preheat the oven to 200°C/400°F/gas mark 6.

Put the saltfish in a saucepan, add cold water to cover, bring to the boil and boil for 5 minutes. Drain off the water and repeat the process.

Drain and flake the fish into an ovenproof dish; cook in the oven for 5 minutes. Remove from the oven and flake into a mixing bowl. Add the oil and stir.

Add the onion, spring onions, garlic, chilli, parsley, thyme and tomatoes and mix thoroughly. Add the lime juice, stir and serve.

TIP

As the saltfish has been thoroughly desalted you may feel the dish lacks salt; taste and add salt if you wish.

ACCRAS DE MORUE

SALTFISH FRITTERS

My mother is the queen of *accras*. Family and friends can arrive at any time of the day and she whips up some fritters so quickly it's crazy. Her secret is that she always has some frozen desalted saltfish in the freezer in case guests arrive. She doesn't have a deep-fat fryer, yet manages to get the oil temperature right every single time.

Makes about 30 fritters

300g/10½oz skinless, boneless dried salted cod
1 onion, very finely chopped
1 spring onion (scallion), very finely chopped
3 garlic cloves, crushed and very finely chopped
2 sprigs flat-leaf parsley, very finely chopped
½ Scotch bonnet chilli, deseeded and very finely chopped
2 eggs, lightly beaten
250g/9oz/2 cups self-raising flour
150ml/5fl oz/ cup water
1 litre/1¾ pints/4 cups sunflower oil

Put the saltfish in a saucepan, add cold water to cover, bring to the boil and boil for 5 minutes. Drain off the water and repeat the process.

Flake the saltfish really finely into a large bowl. Add the onion, spring onion, garlic, parsley and chilli and mix well. Add the eggs and stir until you have a thick paste. Add the flour and mix well, then add the water to make a rich but lumpy batter.

In a deep pan, heat the oil over a medium heat until it reaches 180°C/350°F, or until a cube of bread browns in 3 seconds. Gently drop tablespoonfuls of the batter into the oil and cook for about 30 seconds, turning occasionally, until dark golden brown all over.

Using a slotted spoon, scoop the fritters out of the oil and drain on paper towels. Serve hot, with *sauce chien* (p.146).

CREOLE-STYLE OKRA

Okra, or *gombos* as we call them, were traditionally very common in Creole diets. They now seem to be being consumed less and less. They have a slightly slimy texture but they are very good for you. I loved *gombos* this way. It's so easy to make and works well as a starter or a light dinner for Sunday evening. We consider it a hot salad, but to me it almost feels like a soup; I love slurping the broth.

Serves 4

1kg/2lb 4oz fresh okra
1 onion, very finely chopped
4 spring onions (scallions),
 very finely chopped
3 sprigs parsley, very finely
 chopped
2 thyme sprigs
½ Scotch bonnet chilli, deseeded
1 pinch bicarbonate of soda
 (baking soda)
4 garlic cloves, crushed and very
 finely chopped
juice of 2 limes
salt and freshly ground black
 pepper

Wash the okra and cut off the tips of the stem. Put them in a saucepan with the onion, spring onions, parsley, thyme sprigs and the half chilli. Add water to just cover and add the bicarbonate of soda. Cover and cook over a medium-high heat for 15 minutes.

Using a slotted spoon, lift out the okra into a bowl. Put the saucepan back on the heat and add the garlic, lime juice, salt and pepper. Reduce over a high heat for 2–3 minutes, then pour over the okra. Serve hot.

TIP

Avoid overcooking so the okra isn't too slimy. If you want to make it more like a soup, only boil the sauce for 1 minute after removing the okra.

PRAWN FRITTERS

When one thinks of fritters in the Caribbean, one automatically thinks saltfish. Prawn fritters are probably not quite as popular but they are super easy to make and finding prawns isn't as difficult as finding saltfish. Just make sure your prawns are very big and juicy.

Makes 20–25 fritters

500g/1lb 2oz raw jumbo prawns
    (large shrimp),
    or 600g/1lb 5oz king prawns
2 garlic cloves: 1 crushed,
    1 very finely chopped
juice of 1 lime
salt and freshly ground black
    pepper
200g/7oz/generous 1½ cups plain
    (all-purpose) flour
1 onion, very finely chopped
½ Scotch bonnet chilli, deseeded,
    very finely chopped
3 spring onions (scallions), very
    finely chopped
1 sprig parsley, very finely chopped
150 ml/5 fl oz/⅔ cup water
1 egg, lightly beaten
½ tsp baking powder
1 litre/1¾ pints/4 cups vegetable oil

Peel the prawns and pull off the heads. If they are very big, cut them in half. Put them in a bowl with the crushed garlic clove, lime juice, salt and pepper and marinate for at least 10 minutes.

Put the flour in a large bowl and make a well in the centre. Add the onion, finely chopped garlic, chilli, spring onions and parsley. Add the water and mix to make a batter. Remove the prawns from the marinade, pat them dry and add them to the batter. Add the egg, mix well and leave to rest for at least an hour.

Just before frying add the baking powder and a little more salt and pepper.

In a deep pan, heat the oil over a medium heat until it reaches 180°C/350°F, or until a cube of bread browns in 3 seconds. Making sure there is a prawn in every fritter, gently drop teaspoonfuls of the batter into the oil and cook for about 30 seconds, turning occasionally, until they are deep golden all over.

Using a slotted spoon, scoop the fritters out of the oil and drain on paper towels. Serve hot.

RED SNAPPER BOUDINS

Boudins are a Creole institution. The traditional *boudin* is *boudin noir* (black pudding or blood sausage), which is similar to European black puddings but flavoured with chillies and herbs. Over time, many variations have evolved: crab, saltfish, prawns (shrimp)... My favourite style of *boudin* is fish, made with red snapper. For this recipe it is important that the onions, chilli, garlic and herbs for the sausage filling are chopped extremely finely.

Serves 4–6

1 pack natural sausage casing
   (see Tip, overleaf)
juice of 2 limes
1kg/2lb 4oz snapper fillets
2 Scotch bonnet chillies: 1 whole,
   1 deseeded and very finely
   chopped
4 tbsp vegetable oil
salt and freshly ground black
   pepper
6 garlic cloves: 1 crushed,
   5 very finely chopped
8 spring onions (scallions):
   2 roughly chopped, 6 very
   finely chopped
3 onions: 1 roughly chopped,
   2 very finely chopped
5 sprigs thyme: 2 whole,
   3 very finely chopped
6 sprigs parsley: 2 whole,
   4 very finely chopped
5 bay leaves
1 Caribbean red habanero chilli,
   whole (see p.26)
4 cloves
½ baguette
125ml/4fl oz/½ cup milk
1 tsp ground allspice

Put the sausage casing in a bowl, add cold water to cover and the juice of 1 lime and leave to soak for at least 30 minutes.

Put the fish in a pan with cold water to just cover, the juice of 1 lime, a whole Scotch bonnet, 2 tablespoons of the oil, salt and pepper. Bring to the boil, then reduce the heat and simmer gently for about 5 minutes, until the fish is cooked. Remove the fish from the poaching broth and set aside to cool.

Next, prepare the broth to cook your boudins: fill a large pot with water and add 1 crushed garlic clove, 2 roughly chopped spring onions, a roughly chopped onion, 2 sprigs of thyme and 2 of parsley, the bay leaves, habanero chilli, cloves, salt and pepper. Bring to simmering point and simmer for at least 30 minutes, taking care that the broth never boils.

Once the fish is cool, flake it as finely as possible with your fingers. Put the baguette in a bowl and soak it with cold water, then squeeze out the water with your hands. Purée the bread using your hands and cover with the milk.

Heat the remaining oil in a large saucepan and add the finely chopped onions, spring onions, chilli and garlic for 2 minutes. Add the finely chopped thyme, parsley, allspice and fish, and add salt and pepper to taste. Cook for 3 minutes. Add the bread and milk and cook for another 3 minutes. The filling should be firm. Leave to cool (continued overleaf).

Clean the inside of the sausage casing by running water through it using a funnel. Tie one end of the casing. Using a funnel, pour the fish filling into the casing, ensuring you don't pack it in too tightly. Tie the sausages every 10cm/4in with food-safe string or twist into individual sausages, but do not cut them.

To cook your *boudins* without them touching the bottom of the pot, hook them over a wooden spoon resting across the top of the pot: they should *never* touch the bottom or sides of the pot otherwise they will burst. Place your *boudins* in the pot of broth and cook them over a low heat for 15–20 minutes.

Remove the *boudins* from the pot and leave to cool for about 5 minutes. Cut the individual *boudins* with scissors and serve with a salad, sliced baguette or as part of a Creole platter.

TIP

I use large sausage casing, the same casing you'd use to make black pudding, which is the ancestor of this recipe. A good butcher will advise you: say you are making fish sausages that emulate black pudding! Any good butcher should sell sausage casing, especially if they make their own sausages. Alternatively, look online. Check the instructions: some need to be soaked for 2 hours before use. Some can be kept in the fridge for several months.

GREEN MANGO SOUSKAÏ

I love green mangoes; the sour taste works fabulously with chilli and lime. This is a classic from Martinique. *Souskaï* is the name of both the dish and the technique of macerating fruits in a savoury vinaigrette of lime, garlic, salt and chilli.

Serves 4

2 large green mangoes
1 garlic clove, crushed and very
    finely chopped
2 red bird's-eye chillies,
    very finely chopped
juice of 3 limes
1 tbsp sunflower oil
2 sprigs parsley, finely chopped
salt

Peel the mangoes with a potato peeler (this will ensure you don't waste any of the flesh). Coarsely grate the flesh into a mixing bowl. Add the garlic, chillies, lime juice, oil and parsley. Add salt to taste and stir. Cover with clingfilm (plastic wrap) and leave in the refrigerator for at least 1 hour before serving.

If you like, you can add some diced fresh pineapple.

TIP

You can buy green mangoes from Asian markets and grocery shops. If you can't find them, use an unripe mango from your local supermarket: the flesh will be harder, even if there's sweetness to it.

TARTE À LA MORUE

SALTFISH TART

In every Caribbean household you will find a piece of saltfish hidden somewhere in a cupboard or, in my mum's case, in the freezer. It's just one of the ingredients that, across the region, people invariably use. Although fritters are the most well known usage, saltfish tart is a common feature of the Creole table, especially at a *didiko* (Creole brunch) or for dinner on Sunday when not having soup.

Serves 4–6

400g/14oz skinless, boneless dried salted cod
4 tbsp sunflower oil, plus extra for greasing
4 onions, very finely chopped
5 garlic cloves, crushed and very finely chopped
½ Scotch bonnet chilli, very finely chopped
2 sprigs parsley, very finely chopped
2 sprigs thyme, leaves only
juice of 1 lime
300ml/10fl oz/1¼ cups crème fraîche
2 eggs
200g/7oz shortcrust pastry dough
150g/5½oz Gruyère cheese, grated

Preheat the oven to 180°C/350°F/gas mark 4. Line a 26cm/10½in fluted tart tin with greaseproof (wax) paper and brush lightly with oil.

Put the saltfish in a saucepan, add cold water to cover, bring to the boil and boil for 5 minutes. Drain and leave to cool. Flake the fish.

Heat 2 tablespoons of the oil in a frying pan (skillet) and cook the onions, garlic, chilli, parsley and thyme until softened. Add the flaked fish, lime juice and the remaining oil and cook for 2 minutes.

In a mixing bowl, beat the crème fraîche with the eggs. Add the fish mixture and mix to combine.

On a lightly floured surface, roll out the pastry and line the prepared tart tin. Prick the pastry all over with a fork. Place it in the oven for about 2–3 minutes.

Remove the pastry shell from the oven and pour in the fish mixture. Sprinkle the cheese on top and return to the oven for 25 minutes, until golden and cooked. Serve hot.

TIP

If you have small tartlet tins, make individual tartlets instead and serve with salad for a light dinner.

CREOLE MEAT PIES

These little meat pies are seen at *every* party throughout the Christmas season. Traditionally, they are made with pork, as are most of the savoury foods eaten during that time. However, nowadays these little pies are something we enjoy all year round, filled with saltfish, beef or even conch, and you'll see them in bakeries and at markets.

Makes 20 small pies

2 tbsp sunflower oil
200g/7oz minced (ground) pork or beef
2 garlic cloves, very finely chopped
½ red habanero chilli, very finely chopped
3 spring onions (scallions), very finely chopped
3 sprigs thyme, leaves only, very finely chopped
2 sprigs parsley, very finely chopped
½ tsp ground allspice
½ tsp mixed spice
salt and freshly ground black pepper
300g/10½oz chilled puff pastry dough
1 egg yolk, beaten with 1 tsp semi-skimmed (lowfat) milk

Preheat the oven to 180°C/350°F/gas mark 4. Line a large baking sheet (or two smaller ones) with baking parchment.

Heat the oil in a frying pan (skillet) over a medium–high heat and brown the meat. Add the garlic, chilli, spring onions, thyme, parsley, allspice, mixed spice, salt and pepper and cook for 2–3 minutes. Leave to cool slightly.

Divide the pastry into four. On a lightly floured work surface, roll out the first piece of pastry until it is 2mm/1⁄16 in thick. Using a 10cm/4in round cutter (or a small glass), cut out 10 circles. Place the pastry circles on a lined baking sheet. Put 1 tablespoon of the filling in the middle of each circle; don't overfill. Cover it with another pastry circle. Using the tines of a fork, crimp the edges of the pastry. Repeat until you've used all the pastry and filling.

Using a pastry brush, generously brush egg yolk all over the top of the pies. Bake in the oven for 20 minutes, until golden brown. Serve hot or cold.

FRIED LOBSTER

Lobster never used to be posh food in the Caribbean. My grandfather owned a number of boats, so my mother knew everything about the sea and its food. She tells me that lobsters used to be given away for free by fishermen, since they got caught in their nets and weren't seen as being of value. Today, lobster is very sought after and catching it is highly regulated as it is becoming increasingly rare. When it's in season, you'll find simple charcoal-grilled lobster in the islands' restaurants; this recipe is a quick and easy alternative to try at home.

Serves 4

4 raw lobster tails, peeled
3 limes: 1 squeezed, 2 cut into
    wedges
3 garlic cloves, crushed and
    very finely chopped
1 Scotch bonnet chilli,
    very finely chopped
2 sprigs thyme, leaves only
salt and freshly ground black
    pepper
1 egg
1 tbsp coconut milk
4 tbsp cayenne pepper
1 tbsp allspice
150g/5½oz/generous 1 cup maize
    flour (fine cornmeal)
500ml/18fl oz/2 cups sunflower oil

Marinate the lobster tails with the juice of 1 lime, the garlic, chilli, thyme, salt and pepper for at least an hour.

Cut the lobster tails into 2cm/¾in pieces and pat dry with paper towels. In a bowl, beat the egg with the coconut milk. In another bowl, mix the cayenne pepper with the allspice. Place the maize flour in another bowl.

Heat the oil in a frying pan (skillet) over a medium heat.

Coat the lobster pieces in the beaten egg, then the pepper, then in cornmeal. Place them gently into the hot oil and fry for 2 minutes, turning with tongs or a slotted spoon, until golden. Drain on paper towels. Serve immediately, with lime wedges or hot creole sauce (p.146).

TIP

If maize flour is difficult to find, you can use plain (all-purpose) flour instead.

COCONUT SLAW

Coconut is my favourite fruit in the world. I love it because it's so versatile: from starter to dessert, the possibilities are endless.

I created this recipe because I love coconut souskay – a traditional Martinique recipe – but always felt it lacked something, a bit of a kick, creaminess, texture... This recipe is one of my guests' favourite, always on the request list for menus at my supper clubs.

Serves 4

1 coconut
¼ carrot, coarsely grated
1 small piece (about 3cm/1in) fresh ginger, finely grated
¼ Scotch bonnet chilli, very finely chopped (optional)
salt
1 lime
4 tbsp coconut milk

Break the husk of the coconut and scoop out the meat. Wash the meat and pat dry with paper towels. Coarsely grate the coconut meat into a mixing bowl.

Add the carrot, ginger and chilli and season with salt to taste. Squeeze in the lime juice, add the coconut milk and stir to mix evenly. Cover with clingfilm (plastic wrap) and place in the refrigerator for 1 hour before serving.

Shown here served with smoked herring chiquetaille (see p.58).

CHIKTAY D'HARENG SAUR

SMOKED HERRING CHIQUETAILLE

Smoked herring is one of my favourite foods in the world. Whenever I go home and my mum asks me what I want her to make, I request smoked herring. She doesn't understand why. I like the saltiness, the smoky taste, the dryness of the flesh. This is very easy to make, and I love it on a slice of baguette griddled with olive oil, with finely chopped tomatoes and fresh rocket (arugula), bruschetta style. Pictured on previous page.

Serves 4

2 smoked herring
1 lime, halved
1 sprig thyme
1 or 2 Caribbean red habanero
   chillies
1 onion, chopped
3 garlic cloves, crushed
2 sprigs parsley
2 tbsp sunflower oil

First prepare your herring: slice the belly of the fish open and check if there is an egg pocket – if so, discard it. Clean the fish in cold water, then put them in a saucepan, add cold water to cover, bring to the boil and boil for 5 minutes.

Drain off the water and cover with fresh cold water, add the juice of ½ lime and the thyme, and a whole chilli if you like (it's optional). Boil for another 5 minutes.

Drain the herring and remove the flesh from the bones, taking care to pick out every single bone. Flake the fish with your fingertips until it is completely shredded.

Blitz the onion, garlic, parsley and a chilli in a food processor and add to the herring.

Squeeze in the rest of the lime, stir, add the oil and stir again, then serve.

TIP

For a party, you could serve this stuffed in tomatoes, having scooped out their flesh. Cherry tomatoes look and taste great.

YAM CROQUETTES

Yam is one of those things that was part of my diet growing up in the Caribbean but isn't always the most exciting to cook with. Yam gratin and boiled yam were the two ways we had them regularly. These croquettes are my way of making yam a tad more exciting, with an interesting flavour combination that includes coconut.

Serves 4

500g/1lb 2oz yellow yam
3 tbsp coconut milk
1 egg, lightly beaten
1 sprig parsley, very finely chopped
1 sprig thyme, leaves only
1 spring onion (scallion),
   very finely chopped
¼ Scotch bonnet chilli,
   very finely chopped
1 garlic clove, very finely chopped
20g/¾ oz/1½ tbsp butter, softened
salt and freshly ground black
   pepper
4 tbsp plain (all-purpose) flour
500ml/18fl oz/2 cups vegetable oil

Peel the yam, then cut it into small pieces (about 3cm/1in) and boil until soft when pierced with a knife. Drain and mash the yam with a fork, adding the coconut milk to make a coarse purée. Stir in the egg, herbs, spring onion, chilli and garlic. Add the butter, and season with salt and pepper to taste.

Shape the mixture into balls the size of an egg, roll them in flour and flatten them between the palms of your hands.

Heat the oil in a frying pan (skillet) over a medium heat. Place the fritters gently into the hot oil and pan-fry, turning once, until browned on both sides. Drain on paper towels. Serve hot, with a salad.

TIP

Yellow and white yams look similar on the outside, although yellow yam tends to be more hairy, so the best thing to do is ask the shopkeeper for yellow yam. If yellow yams are not available, you can substitute white yams or sweet potatoes.

CHRISTOPHINE AU GRATIN

CHOCHO GRATIN

This classic of Creole cuisine makes a rather bland squash taste delicious: the watery flesh takes on new life when mixed with bacon. Be very gentle with the chocho skin, as it breaks quite easily.

Serves 4

2 large chochos (chayote/
   christophines)
salt and freshly ground black
   pepper
1 tbsp sunflower oil
1 tbsp butter
175g/6oz smoked lardons
1 onion, very finely chopped
3 spring onions (scallions), very
   finely chopped
1 garlic clove, crushed and very
   finely chopped
1 sprig parsley, chopped
3 tbsp crème fraîche
1 pinch mixed spice
30g/1oz Emmental cheese, grated

Cut the chochos in half and remove the cores. Place them in a pan of lightly salted boiling water and boil for 45 minutes until the flesh is very soft. Drain and leave to cool.

Preheat the oven to 180°C/350°F/gas mark 4.

Using a knife, gently remove the fibrous part around the core of the chochos. Using a spoon, gently scoop out the flesh, leaving the skin intact. Mash the flesh with a potato masher or a fork and set aside.

Heat the oil and butter in a frying pan (skillet) and cook the bacon, onion, spring onions, garlic and parsley until the onion has softened.

Add the chocho flesh, crème fraîche, mixed spice and most of the cheese, and season with salt and pepper to taste.

Place the chocho skins in a baking dish and fill them with the stuffing. Sprinkle the remaining cheese on top. Place in the oven for about 15 minutes, until golden. Serve hot.

TIP

These are slightly large, but can be served as part of a Creole platter.

SALADE DE CHRISTOPHINE

CHOCHO SALAD

Many of my students arrive at my classes saying they hate chocho (if they have had it before). They have childhood memories of chocho in a slimy soup, or boiled with no seasoning. This recipe never fails to reconcile them with chocho. It's just a simple salad, but most people don't even know you can eat it raw. Once they've tried this, it becomes a go-to recipe when they want an alternative to their usual salads.

Serves 4

2 chochos (chayote/christophines)
juice of 1 lime
salt and freshly ground black
   pepper
2 tbsp sunflower oil
1 garlic clove, very finely chopped
¼ Scotch bonnet chilli, deseeded
   and very finely chopped

Peel the chochos with a potato peeler and cut them in half. Grate the flesh and stop grating once you reach the core. Throw away the core.

In a bowl, make a vinaigrette with the lime juice, salt, pepper, oil, garlic and chilli.

Cover the chocho with the vinaigrette and toss gently. Place in the refrigerator for at least 15 minutes before serving.

CORNED BEEF MINI BOKITS

This is what I call a 'hard times recipe'. Processed meat and fried dough wouldn't strike anyone as gourmet food, but they are delicious. This is the type of food you'd cook if you were trapped in your house during a hurricane or in the aftermath of a flood after a tropical downpour.

Makes 15–20 mini bokits

Bokits
½ tbsp fast-action dried
   (active dry) yeast
1 tsp salt
3 tbsp milk
200ml/7fl oz/scant 1 cup water
375g/13oz plain (all-purpose) flour,
   plus extra for dusting
1 litre/1¾ pints/4 cups vegetable oil

Filling
3 tbsp vegetable oil
1 can (about 350g/12oz) corned
   beef (canned pressed beef),
   chopped
1 onion, very finely chopped
1 spring onion (scallion),
   very finely chopped
3 garlic cloves, crushed and
   very finely chopped
1 Scotch bonnet chilli, deseeded,
   very finely chopped
2 sprigs thyme, leaves only
2 sprigs parsley, very finely
   chopped
1 tbsp white vinegar
salt and freshly ground black
   pepper

To make the bokits: in a small bowl, dissolve the yeast and the salt in the milk. Pour the yeasty milk into a large mixing bowl and add the water and flour. Knead for at least 10 minutes, until the dough is smooth and elastic. Shape into a ball, place in an oiled bowl, cover and leave in a warm place to rise for at least 5 hours.

To make the filling, heat the oil in a frying pan (skillet) over a medium-high heat. Add the corned beef and cook for about 2 minutes. Add the onion, spring onion, garlic, chilli, thyme and parsley and cook, stirring frequently, for 3–4 minutes until thoroughly cooked and slightly crisp.

Add the vinegar and stir to deglaze the pan. Add salt and pepper to taste, cook for another minute and then remove from the heat.

To shape the bokits, pinch a small ball of dough about 5cm/2in wide and 2mm/⅟₁₆ in thick. On a lightly floured work surface, roll out the dough to a thin circle about 15cm/6in in diameter. Place 2 tablespoons of the corned beef mixture on one side of the circle and fold the other half over the corned beef. Press down the edges. Repeat until you have used all the filling.

In a deep pan, heat the oil over a medium heat until it reaches 180°C/350°F, or until a cube of bread browns in 3 seconds. Gently lower a bokit into the oil and cook for about 1 minute on each side, until golden and crisp. Scoop out of the oil and drain on paper towels. Eat while still hot.

PWASSON É FWIDMÈ
FISH AND SEAFOOD

◆◆◆◆◆◆◆◆◆

Caribbean Creole cuisine showcases its diverse influences in the arena of main dishes, which we call *pla'*. Some of the recipes are seasonal because of the availability of the ingredients, some because they are so closely linked to specific holidays. Others are invariably consumed at least once a week in Creole households.

Fish and seafood tend to dominate, in many forms: stewed, grilled, fried, poached, and cooked in rice – you're spoiled for choice. The Amerindian heritage is seen in the grilled fish and seafood, the influence of the French in the fragrant broths used for poaching. Saltfish was introduced by the Portuguese – and there are rice dishes that will remind you of Spanish paella. *Dombrés* (see p.82), or dumplings, are a truly Creole creation, evolving at a time when slaves and field workers needed energy-rich foods to add to whatever fish or meat they could get their hands on.

PRAWN BLAFF

Some say blaff gets its name from the sound fish and seafood make when thrown into the fragrant broth: 'blaff'! Others think it derives from the French word *blafard*, which means pale, because of how colourless the sauce is. This simple dish has its roots in French cuisine, with a very aromatic broth that tastes wonderful served with simply boiled roots, such as sweet potatoes, yam or plantains.

Serves 4

1kg/2lb 4oz raw jumbo tiger prawns (large shrimp)
2 limes
3 garlic cloves, crushed
salt and freshly ground black pepper
2 tbsp sunflower oil
2 onions, chopped
1 clove
3 spring onions (scallions), chopped
1 bay leaf
2 sprigs thyme, leaves only
500ml/18fl oz/2 cups water
1 habanero chilli
2 sprigs parsley, chopped

Marinate the prawns in their shells with the juice of 1 lime, 1 crushed garlic clove, salt and pepper for at least 2 hours.

Heat the oil in a pot over a medium heat, add the onions, clove, spring onions, bay leaf and thyme and cook for 3 minutes. Add the water, the whole chilli and the juice of ½ a lime and cook for 5 minutes, stirring occasionally, taking care not to burst the chilli.

Add the prawns with their marinade, along with the remaining garlic, the juice of the remaining ½ lime, parsley, salt and pepper to taste. Cover and cook for another 5 minutes. Remove the chilli and serve hot, in bowls.

OUASSOUS FLAMBÉ

FLAMBÉ PRAWNS

I've always loved the wow factor of flambé. It mesmerized me the first day I was allowed to flambé food, which happened to be prawns, so this is a milestone recipe for me.

Serves 4–6

1kg/2lb 4oz raw king prawn tails
    (large shrimp)
juice of 1 lime
75ml/2½fl oz/5 tbsp white rum
4 tbsp vegetable oil
1 onion, sliced
2 garlic cloves, crushed
2 sprigs parsley, finely chopped
1 sprig thyme, leaves only
1 bay leaf
salt and freshly ground black
    pepper
2 tbsp brown sugar
4 tbsp aged rum

Marinate the prawns with the lime juice, half the white rum, 2 tablespoons of the oil, onion, garlic, parsley, thyme, bay leaf, salt and pepper for at least 2 hours.

Thread the prawns onto small skewers.

Heat the remaining oil in a large frying pan (skillet) over a medium heat and cook the prawns for 3 minutes on each side.

Sprinkle the sugar over the prawns and – standing well back as the flames leap up – immediately pour in the remaining white rum and the aged rum and flambé, either by tilting the pan (if you have a gas hob) or by holding a match near to the pan (on an electric hob). As soon as the flames die down, slide the prawns off the skewers onto a serving platter and pour the rum sauce over. Serve immediately.

OCTOPUS FRICASSÉE

The local variety of octopus in the seas of Guadeloupe and Martinique is called *chatrou*. **If you ask for anything else they won't know what you're talking about. When I was growing up, my father cooked this dish just for me, since none of my siblings nor my mother like it. I love it with plain boiled white rice and a large piece of chilli on the side. I'll never get enough!**

Serves 4

1kg/2lb 4oz octopus, gutted, cleaned and beak removed
3 limes
salt and freshly ground black pepper
3 garlic cloves, crushed and very finely chopped
2 sprigs thyme
2 large bay leaves
4 tbsp sunflower oil
1 onion, very finely chopped
4 spring onions (scallions), very finely chopped
2 cloves
1 habanero chilli
3 large ripe tomatoes, chopped
200ml/7fl oz/scant 1 cup water
2 sprigs flat-leaf parsley, chopped

Rinse the octopus thoroughly in water. Use some newspaper to clean it and remove all the slime. Ensure you get rid of all the ink. Squeeze a lime over the octopus. Wrap the octopus in clingfilm (plastic wrap) and pound it with a mallet or a rolling pin (or the bottom of a heavy saucepan) for about 5 minutes.

Cut the octopus into chunky pieces (3–4cm/about 1½in) and marinate with salt, pepper, the juice of ½ a lime, 1 garlic clove, 1 sprig of thyme and 1 bay leaf. Place in the refrigerator for at least 2 hours, or preferably overnight.

Heat 3 tablespoons of the oil in a pot over a medium heat, add the octopus and its marinade and cook it for a few minutes until it releases a pinkish liquid. Add the remaining garlic, the onion, spring onions, cloves and 1 sprig of thyme and cook, covered, over a low heat for 10 minutes.

Add the juice of 1 lime and the whole chilli, the tomatoes and water. Cover and cook over a medium heat for 25 minutes.

Once the liquid has reduced slightly, add 1 tablespoon oil and the parsley. Taste and adjust the seasoning. Add the juice of ½ a lime, cover the pot and cook over a high heat for 5 minutes. Stir occasionally, taking care not to burst the chilli.

Remove the chilli. Serve hot, with stewed red kidney beans (p.128) and boiled basmati rice.

LOBSTER FRICASSÉE

I love lobster. It's hard to believe that, back when tourism wasn't so developed in Guadeloupe and Martinique, fishermen would offer lobsters free or give them to customers instead of change. Nowadays, lobster is synonymous with a fancy meal when you have something to celebrate.

Serves 4

1kg/2lb 4oz raw lobster tails with
  shell on
2 limes
salt and freshly ground black
  pepper
3 tbsp sunflower oil
1 onion, very finely chopped
2 spring onions (scallions),
  very finely chopped
2 sprigs thyme
2 sprigs parsley, chopped
2 pinches ground allspice
1 bay leaf
2 garlic cloves, crushed
3 ripe tomatoes, chopped
1 tbsp tomato purée (paste)
125ml/4fl oz/½ cup water
1 Scotch bonnet chilli

Marinate the lobster tails with the juice of 1 lime, salt and pepper for at least an hour.

Lift the lobster out of its marinade and pat dry. Heat the oil in a pot over a medium heat, add the lobster and cook for about 3–4 minutes. Add the onion, spring onions, thyme sprigs, parsley, allspice, bay leaf and garlic and cook for an additional 3–4 minutes.

Add the tomatoes and tomato purée and stir. Season with salt and pepper to taste and add the water, the whole chilli and the juice of 1 lime. Cover and cook over a low heat for 30 minutes, stirring occasionally, taking not to burst the chilli.

Remove the chilli and thyme. Serve hot with rice.

FISH COURT BOUILLON

Creole fish court bouillon is the recipe every cook in the Caribbean has to master. It's a tomato-based, very spicy broth in which parrotfish, snappers and other colourful Caribbean fish are poached until tender. It can be made with just one type of fish, or a mix of different fish.

Most cooks in the French Caribbean keep some achiote seeds in a bottle of vegetable oil to use for fish court bouillon. The seeds give the oil a subtle, peppery, nutty flavour and a warm red colour. Unrefined palm oil can be used instead; it has a reddish colour but a slightly different taste.

Serves 4

1kg/2lb 4oz red snapper, whole parrotfish, red butterfish or pink sea bream steaks, scaled and cleaned
3 garlic cloves, crushed
1 bay leaf
3 limes
salt and freshly ground black pepper
1 tbsp sunflower oil
250ml/9fl oz/1 cup water
3 tbsp achiote-infused oil (alternatively use unrefined palm oil)
1 onion, very finely chopped
3 sprigs thyme
3 sprigs parsley, chopped
3 spring onions (scallions), very finely chopped
3 large ripe tomatoes, chopped
2 tbsp tomato purée (paste)
1 Scotch bonnet chilli

If using parrotfish or any other small fish, leave them whole. If using red snapper cut them in half. In a large mixing bowl, combine 1 crushed garlic clove, the bay leaf, the juice of 2 limes, salt and pepper, the sunflower oil and 125ml/4fl oz/½ cup water. Add all the fish and marinate for at least 2 hours.

Heat the achiote oil in a large pot over a medium heat and cook the onion, thyme sprigs, parsley, spring onions and the remaining garlic for about a minute. Add the tomatoes and cook for 2 minutes. Add 125ml/4fl oz/½ cup water and stir in the tomato purée. Cook for another 2 minutes.

Add the fish and marinade and put them in the pot – they will cook at different times, so add firmer and larger fish first, smaller fish last – ensuring the sauce covers them: if not, add more water. Add the whole chilli. Cover the pot and cook over a low heat for 10 minutes for most small fish, 15 minutes for snapper and 20 minutes if using sea bream steak.

Season with salt and pepper and lime juice to taste. Remove the chilli and bay leaf. Serve hot with root vegetables or ground provisions (see glossary on p.186), which could include boiled plantains, yam, breadfruit or sweet potato.

GREEN BANANA AND SALTFISH

I love the simplicity of this dish. In Guadeloupe, the people you'll see ordering this for their lunch are often the big guys: truck drivers, builders, people with tough jobs working under the very hot Caribbean sun. *Ti' punch* (p.24) is de rigueur with this dish. It's a rustic everyday meal, served in large portions – one of my favourites.

Serves 4

4 thick salted cod cutlets
2 green bananas per person
6 tablespoons sunflower oil
2–3 garlic cloves, crushed
1 bay leaf
4 sprigs thyme
2 sprigs parsley, chopped
juice of 1½ limes
1 habanero chilli, deseeded and finely chopped
2 onions, sliced
salt and freshly ground black pepper
1 large cucumber, peeled, grated
1 large avocado

TIP

Traditionally, we like to have a habanero chilli and a lime wedge on the side to adjust the flavours to individual taste, and some sunflower oil to pour over the green bananas. We crush everything together, from the fish to the avocado, and although it's a messy plate, the flavours combine perfectly.

Put the salted cod in a saucepan, add cold water to cover, bring to the boil and boil for 5 minutes. Drain off the water and repeat the process. Drain.

Wash the green bananas thoroughly. Cut off both ends and make a 1cm/½in deep slit lengthwise; once boiled, the skin will drop off easily. Boil the green bananas for 30 minutes.

Meanwhile, heat 2 tablespoons oil in a wide, shallow pot over a medium heat. Add the cod and cook for about 2 minutes on each side. Add the garlic, bay leaf, thyme sprigs, chopped parsley, juice of 1 lime and ½ the chilli and cook for 5 minutes. Reduce the heat and add 4 tablespoons water. Cook for 5 minutes over a low heat, then set aside.

In a frying pan (skillet), heat 4 tablespoons oil over a medium heat, add the onions and cook for about 10 minutes, until they become translucent. Add a little salt to taste, a pinch of pepper and the remaining chilli. Tip the onions over the cod.

Squeeze the juice of ½ lime over the cucumbers. Peel the avocado and cut into small cubes.

Drain the green bananas and serve on a plate with the cod, cucumber and avocado.

HACHIS D'IGNAME ET DE MORUE

CREOLE PARMENTIER: YAM AND SALTFISH

My father was anti-potatoes. It was almost like a vendetta. Potatoes were not likely to have grown on our ground, so he felt we should use local roots instead. We did have potatoes from time to time but yams would have been his first choice. He planted them in our garden and they were massive. This is one way we'd have them.

Serves 4–6

1kg/2lb 4oz yam
salt and freshly ground black
    pepper
4 tbsp sunflower oil
1 onion, very finely chopped
3 spring onions (scallions), very
    finely chopped
4 garlic cloves, crushed
100ml/3½fl oz/scant ½ cup canned
    coconut milk
50g/1¾oz/4 tbsp butter, at room
    temperature, plus extra for
    greasing
300g/10½oz saltfish chiquetaille
    (p.41)
5 tbsp fresh or dried breadcrumbs
125g/4½oz Emmental cheese,
    grated

Peel the yam and cut into chunks. Place in a pan of lightly salted boiling water and boil for 30 minutes. Drain and mash.

Preheat the oven to 180°C/350°F/gas mark 4. Butter a large gratin dish.

Heat the oil in a saucepan over a medium heat, add the onion, spring onions and garlic and cook until softened. Add the yam purée and stir to mix, then add the coconut milk, butter, and salt and pepper to taste.

Spread half of the yam purée over the bottom of the gratin dish, cover with the saltfish chiquetaille and then with the rest of the yam purée. Sprinkle the breadcrumbs and cheese evenly over the surface. Bake for about 15 minutes, until the top is golden. Serve hot.

FISH BLAFF

'Blaff'. That's the sound fish makes when you drop it into the broth. This is so simple it is one of the first recipes I ever learned to make, when I was around eight years old. Water, herbs, spices and fish. Anyone can do this.

Serves 4

1kg/2lb 4oz fish, such as pink sea
   bream or red mullet, scaled
   and cleaned
4 garlic cloves, crushed
5 bay leaves
juice of 6 limes
salt and freshly ground black
   pepper
2 tbsp sunflower oil
1 onion, sliced
3 spring onions (scallions),
   chopped
3 sprigs thyme
3 sprigs parsley, chopped
1 Scotch bonnet chilli
500ml/18fl oz/2 cups water

Marinate the fish with 2 of the garlic cloves, 2 bay leaves, the juice of 4 limes, and salt and pepper for at least 2 hours.

Heat the oil in a pot over a medium heat, add the onion, the remaining garlic, spring onions, thyme sprigs, parsley, the remaining 3 bay leaves, the whole chilli, salt and pepper and cook for 2 minutes. Add the water and bring to simmering point. Add the fish and the juice of 2 limes and simmer for 15 minutes.

Taste and adjust the seasoning, remove the chilli and serve hot, in bowls, ideally with boiled plantains.

COCONUT MILK RED SNAPPER

I love fish. Growing up on an island that is known for its beautiful seas and outstanding coral life, I have many memories of going to the market with my father very early in the morning and buying fish that was still alive in the fishermen's boat. Although they were happy to scale and clean the fish, my father insisted that my brother and I did this, so we would learn how to prepare it. It was an exciting learning curve for me to understand the anatomy of the different fish – and it really made me appreciate how wonderful fish can be.

Serves 4

4 small red snapper, scaled, cleaned and filleted
salt and freshly ground black pepper
5 spring onions (scallions), very finely chopped
1 onion, very finely chopped
½ Scotch bonnet chilli, very finely chopped
3 garlic cloves, crushed and very finely chopped
5 limes
2 tbsp sunflower oil
200ml/7fl oz/scant 1 cup canned coconut milk
2 tbsp finely chopped parsley

Cut the snapper fillets into thin strips and place them in a bowl. Grind over some salt and pepper. Add the spring onions, onion, chilli and garlic. Squeeze 2 limes over the fish. Using your hands, mix the fish gently with the marinade. Cover and leave in the refrigerator for at least 3 hours.

Take the bowl out of the refrigerator 10 minutes before you are ready to serve.

Heat the oil in a frying pan (skillet) over a medium–high heat. Remove the fish from the marinade and pat dry with paper towels. Put the snapper into the oil and cook for 2 minutes on each side.

Add the coconut milk to the pan and cook for 2 minutes.

Divide the fish among four serving plates, pour some of the coconut milk over and sprinkle with chopped parsley.

DOMBRÉS AND PRAWNS

Dombrés are very similar to dumplings and take their name from the very basic bread the English used to throw their prisoners, known as 'the damned', who they kept in the caves below their forts. It started off being called 'damned bread', and soon became *dombrés*. The dumplings, added to stews made with red kidney beans and pigs' tails, crab, prawns (shrimp) or crayfish, provided energy for the field workers. Despite their poverty, the slaves and labourers showed great ingenuity in making their dishes interesting and tasty. If they worked near a river or the sea, they were able to catch crayfish, large prawns or land crabs – and anyother shellfish they could get their hands on: it all went into the pot with the *dombrés*.

Serves 4

400g/14oz raw king prawns (large shrimp) in their shells
3 spring onions (scallions), chopped
1 large onion, very finely chopped
1 tomato, diced
1 x 400g can chopped tomatoes
2 garlic cloves, crushed
700ml/24fl oz/scant 3 cups water
3 pinches salt
juice of 1 lime
1 Scotch bonnet chilli
3 sprigs parsley, chopped

Dombré dough
450g/1lb/scant 4 cups plain (all-purpose) flour
250ml/9fl oz/1 cup cold water
1 tsp salt

First make the *dombré* dough. Put the flour in a large mixing bowl and make a well in the centre. Add the water and salt to the well and then mix and knead until you have a ball of dough that does not stick to your fingers.

Pinch off a piece of dough about 2cm/¾in in diameter and roll it into a small ball. Continue making small balls until you've used up all the dough.

Heat the oil in a large pot over a medium heat. Throw in the prawns and cook until pink. Add all the onions and cook for about 5 minutes, until softened.

Add the fresh tomato, canned tomatoes and garlic and cook for 5 minutes.

Add the cold water and salt and bring to simmering point. Add the *dombrés* dough balls to the sauce. Squeeze in the lime juice, add the whole chilli, cover the pan and cook over a low heat for 30 minutes, until the sauce thickens.

Remove the chilli, add the chopped parsley, and serve.

CRAB MATÉTÉ

Easter is one of the biggest celebrations in the French Caribbean. My father used to start preparing for it from the first week of Lent. We would go to Morne à l'Eau – a small town in Guadeloupe renowned for having the best crabs – and would buy about 15 of them. We farmed the crabs for a month, feeding them chillies, spring onions (scallions), garlic and parsley. This flavoured them from within, ensuring the flesh was as tasty as could be.

From crabmeat rum punch to crab matété, crab callaloo and *dombrés* – crabs are at the centre of the celebrations. There's even a traditional Creole song about the benefits of crab matété, claiming it is where Creole men get their 'strength'.

Serves 4

4 fresh whole crabs, or 12 crab claws
3 limes
4 large garlic cloves, crushed and very finely chopped
2 Scotch bonnet chillies, deseeded and very finely chopped
salt and freshly ground black pepper
4 tbsp vegetable oil
3 slices of smoked bacon slab, cut into small cubes, or 300g/10½oz smoked lardons
1 large onion, very finely chopped
2 spring onions (scallions), very finely chopped
2 sprigs parsley, chopped
2 sprigs thyme
4 large ripe tomatoes, diced
3 cloves
2 bay leaves
1 tsp Colombo powder
250g/9oz/generous 1¼ cups long-grain rice, washed twice

Clean your crabs with a small scrubbing brush. If using whole crabs, pull the shells away from the bodies. Discard the shells, the small stomach sac just behind the crab's mouth and the soft grey gills. Cut one of the limes into quarters. Clean the bodies with cold water and use the juice of ¼ lime to clean each crab, rubbing the squeezed lime wedge over the body. Using a heavy knife, chop the crab bodies into quarters, keeping two or three legs attached to each quarter. Marinate the crab pieces or claws with the juice of 1 lime, 1 garlic clove, 1 chilli, salt and pepper. Place in the refrigerator for at least 4 hours.

Heat 2 tablespoons of the oil in a large pot over a low heat, add the bacon and cook for about 2 minutes. Lift the crabs out of their marinade (strain the marinade and set aside) and add to the pot, along with the onion, spring onions, parsley and thyme sprigs and cook for 2 minutes.

Add the tomatoes, cloves, bay leaves, the remaining garlic and chilli, some pepper and a little salt. Add the marinade. Cover and cook over a low heat for 10–15 minutes.

(method continues overleaf)

Add the Colombo powder and the rest of the oil, then add the rice. Mix thoroughly to coat the rice evenly in the sauce. Squeeze in the juice of the remaining lime. Mix gently and add water if necessary, to cover the crab and rice by about 1cm/½in. Season with salt and pepper, cover and cook over a low heat for 15–20 minutes, until the rice is soft, stirring once or twice to ensure the rice doesn't stick to the bottom of the pot and burn. Serve hot.

In my house we served the matété with a lime wedge on the side to squeeze in while eating. We'd also enjoy it with infused rums such as passion fruit punch (p.29).

TIP

Many of the Indian migrants, who arrived around 1862, came from southern India and Ceylon (now Sri Lanka), whose capital city is Colombo, and so this is how their traditional spice mix acquired its name. You can make your own by putting all the following spices in a spice grinder or mortar and pestle and grinding to a fine powder. Sieve it, keep in an airtight container and try to use within 2–3 months:

2 tbsp coriander seeds
2 tbsp ground turmeric
1 tbsp cumin seeds
1 tbsp mustard seeds
½ tbsp fenugreek seeds
1 clove
1 tbsp garlic powder

SALT COD BRANDADE

This recipe has France written all over it. My parents worked very hard running their own successful business, so we children all ate at the school canteen. Salt cod brandade and stewed lentils was my favourite canteen meal. They'd usually serve it on Fridays and I really looked forward to it – real comfort food!

Serves 4

600g/1lb 5oz skinless, boneless dried salted cod
1.5kg/3lb 5oz yam
4 tbsp sunflower oil
1 onion, very finely chopped
3 spring onions (scallions), very finely chopped
3 garlic cloves, very finely chopped
1 sprig thyme, leaves only
2 sprigs parsley, chopped
60g/2¼oz/4½ tbsp butter
250ml/9fl oz/1 cup milk
salt and freshly ground black pepper
60g/2¼oz Gruyère cheese, grated
2 tbsp fresh or dried breadcrumbs

Put the saltfish in a saucepan, add cold water to cover, bring to the boil and boil for 5 minutes. Drain off the water and repeat the process. Blend the cod in a food processor for about 1 minute. Set aside.

Peel the yam and cut into small chunks. Place in a pan of lightly salted boiling water and boil for 30 minutes or until completely soft. Drain and mash with a fork. Set aside.

Preheat the oven to 200°C/400°F/gas mark 6.

Heat the oil in a pot over a medium heat, add the onion, spring onions, garlic, thyme and parsley and cook until softened. Add the cod and stir. Add the yam, butter and milk and stir vigorously. Season with salt and pepper to taste. Spread evenly in a gratin dish and sprinkle the breadcrumbs and cheese over the surface. Bake for about 15 minutes, until the top is golden. Serve hot.

Suggestion: Serve with stewed lentils (p.126).

CREOLE FRIED FISH

What I love the most about this dish are the fried onions and chilli we traditionally put on top of it. This recipe works best with snapper.

Serves 4

4 small snappers, scaled and
  cleaned
salt and freshly ground black
  pepper
2 garlic cloves, very finely chopped
juice of 1 lime, plus lime wedges,
  to serve
2 Scotch bonnet chillies:
  1 chopped, 1 sliced (optional)
about 600ml/20fl oz/2½ cups
  vegetable oil
about 100g/3½oz/generous ¾ cup
  plain (all-purpose) flour
1 tsp ground allspice
1 onion, thinly sliced

Marinate the fish in the refrigerator overnight with salt and pepper, the garlic, lime juice, chopped chilli, and 2 tablespoons of the oil.

Remove the fish from its marinade and pat dry with paper towels.

Put the flour on a large plate and mix with the allspice, salt and pepper. Roll each fish in the flour.

Heat about 500ml/18fl oz/2 cups of the oil in a large frying pan (skillet) over a medium heat. Add the fish and cook until golden and crisp. Drain on paper towels.

In a separate saucepan, heat 5 tablespoons of vegetable oil and fry the onion until softened, together with the sliced chilli if you're brave.

To serve, put a whole fish on each plate and cover with the fried onions. Serve with a lime wedge on the side.

MEAT AND POULTRY

Many of these meat dishes are authentic recipes you could only
have tried if they were cooked for you by a local. They are often
not sexy on the plate but are definitely what I would call
Creole soul food: one-pot, slow-cooked stews that reveal
their African heritage.

Cooking meat Creole style means it's what Europeans would
consider overcooked. But in the tropical climate it is necessary to
cook meats thoroughly to avoid food poisoning. It's stewed for
hours, until it falls off the bones or melts in your mouth.

I remember the first time I was allowed to make a meat stew
for the family Sunday lunch: big responsibility! I was about
13 years old and had decided to make a rabbit ragout. I'd seen my
father make so many of these traditional one-pot stews that
I instinctively knew what to do, so I was happy to get on with it,
and my dad was pretty proud.

CREOLE PORK RAGOUT

This is the cornerstone of the Creole Christmas dinner. This is why the pig was fed every day throughout the year on breadfruit, nice bananas and good guavas, so its meat would be juicy and flavoursome. This is why you spend hours marinating the meat and slow-cooking it. It has to be tender, melt-in-your-mouth and give instant comfort.

Serves 4

700g/1lb 9oz pork shoulder,
   cut into chunks
juice of 2 limes
4 garlic cloves, very finely chopped
2 tsp ground allspice
salt and freshly ground black
   pepper
2 tbsp vegetable oil
2 onions, sliced
2 spring onions (scallions),
   chopped
2 sprigs thyme
2 bay leaves
1 clove
1 Scotch bonnet chilli
125ml/4fl oz/½ cup water

Marinate the pork in the refrigerator overnight with the juice of 1 lime, half the garlic, half the allspice, salt and pepper.

Remove the pork from the marinade and pat dry with paper towels. Heat the oil in a large heavy pot over a medium–high heat, add the pork and cook until browned. Add the onions, spring onions, the remaining allspice, salt and pepper, stir and brown for a few minutes.

Add the juice of 1 lime, the remaining garlic, thyme sprigs, bay leaves, clove, the whole chilli and the water. Cover and cook over a very low heat for 2 hours, until the meat is very tender.

Serve with stewed pigeon peas (p.129) and rice or a vegetable gratin.

BREADFRUIT HOTPOT

This is an African slave recipe, a simple one-pot stew that truly represents the African heritage in Creole food.

Serves 6

3 salted pigs' tails
1 breadfruit
4 tbsp vegetable oil
200g/7oz salted beef, diced
100g/3½oz smoked bacon slab, diced
about 100g/3½oz calabaza (West Indian pumpkin), peeled and cubed
1 onion, chopped
4 spring onions (scallions), chopped
4 garlic cloves, chopped
2 sprigs thyme
1 aji dulce chilli, chopped
1.2 litres/2 pints/4½ cups water
1 bay leaf
1 clove
2 sprigs parsley, chopped
salt and freshly ground black pepper
1 habanero chilli

Clean the pigs' tails in cold water, then put them in a saucepan, add cold water to cover, bring to the boil and boil for 20 minutes.

Cut the breadfruit into four. Peel, remove and discard the core and cut into cubes.

Drain the pigs' tails and cut into pieces through the joints. Pat dry with paper towels.

Heat the oil in a large pot over a medium heat, add the pigs' tails, beef and bacon and brown for 2–3 minutes.

Add the breadfruit, calabaza, onion and spring onions, garlic, thyme, aji dulce chilli and 125ml/4fl oz/½ cup of the water. Stir, then add the remaining water, the bay leaf, clove, parsley, salt, pepper and the whole habanero chilli. Cover the pot and simmer over a low heat for 30–40 minutes, stirring occasionally, taking care not to burst the chilli.

Remove the chilli. Serve hot.

TIP

Salted pigs' tails are a typically Caribbean ingredient; look for them in Afro-Caribbean shops and online.

MUTTON COLOMBO

Like most other islands in the Caribbean, Guadeloupe and Martinique have a traditional curry. Ours is called Colombo. We inherited it from the indentured Indians who arrived to work on the islands after slavery was abolished. It is named after the capital city of Sri Lanka and the same name is used for the particular mix of spices we use for this curry; it's easy to make your own (p.86), but in Guadeloupe and Martinique you will find Colombo on every market stall, every supermarket, in every household's cupboards and on every menu. We make Colombo with chicken, pork, mutton, goat, prawns, shark and even skate. I would go as far as saying it's one of the official dishes of Guadeloupe and Martinique.

Serves 4

1kg/2lb 4oz mutton or goat, cut into chunks
3 garlic cloves, crushed and very finely chopped
6 tbsp Colombo powder (p.86)
salt and freshly ground black pepper
juice of 1 lime
3 tbsp vegetable oil
2 onions, very finely chopped
3 spring onions (scallions), chopped
1 tsp tamarind paste
1 aubergine (eggplant), diced
1 sweet potato (approximately 150g/5½oz), diced
100g/3½oz yam, diced
1 Scotch bonnet chilli
2 sprigs thyme
2 sprigs parsley, chopped

Marinate the meat with 1 garlic clove, 2 tablespoons Colombo powder, salt and pepper, the juice of 1 lime and 1 tablespoon oil for at least 2 hours, or preferably overnight.

Remove the meat from the marinade and pat dry with paper towels. Heat the remaining 2 tablespoons oil in a large heavy pot over a medium–high heat, add the meat and cook, stirring occasionally, until browned.

Add the onions, the remaining garlic, the spring onions, tamarind paste, the remaining Colombo powder and 4 tablespoons of water, then add the aubergine, sweet potato and yam, the whole chilli, thyme, parsley, salt and pepper. Reduce the heat, cover the pot and cook over a low heat for 45 minutes, until the meat is very tender.

Serve hot, with boiled white basmati rice or coconut rice (p.114).

BÉBÉLÉ

I love *bébélé* – tripe with green bananas and *dombrés*. It's a speciality of Marie-Galante, my mother's island, and is usually served at christenings, first communions and weddings. In the UK tripe is often sold pre-cooked and cleaned, but for this recipe you need to start with raw tripe. Ask your butcher for advice.

Serves 4–6

700g/1lb 9oz raw tripe, prepared
3 salted pigs' tails
3 tablespoons vegetable oil
2 onions, finely chopped
9 spring onions (scallions),
   finely chopped
2 bay leaves
6 cloves
2 carrots, peeled and diced
300g/10½oz yam, peeled and diced
2 malangas (eddo) or dasheen
   (taro), peeled and diced
½ breadfruit, peeled and diced
1 slice (about 200g/7oz) of
   calabaza (West Indian pumpkin),
   peeled and diced
3 green bananas, peeled and diced
50g/1¾oz canned green pigeon
   peas, drained
350g/12oz smoked bacon slab,
   diced
3 sprigs parsley, chopped
2 sprigs thyme
3 garlic cloves, crushed
salt and freshly ground black
   pepper
1 habanero chilli
dombré dough, rolled into very
   small balls (p.82)

Starting the day before you want to make this dish, prepare the tripe. Clean thoroughly in cold water, remove any blood vessels and sinews and then soak overnight in lime juice and water.

Clean the pigs' tails in cold water, then put them in a saucepan, add cold water to cover, bring to the boil and boil for 20 minutes. Drain and cut the pigs' tails into pieces through the joints.

Heat 2 tablespoons of the oil in a pot, add the onions and 6 spring onions and cook for 2–3 minutes. Add the tripe and tails, stir and add cold water to cover. Add 1 bay leaf and 1 clove. Cover and simmer gently over a medium–low heat for at least 1½ hours, until the tripe is meltingly tender. Alternatively, cook for 30 minutes in a pressure cooker over a medium heat.

Heat the remaining oil in a large pot over a medium heat, add the carrots and cook for 2–3 minutes. Add all the remaining vegetables and stir well. Add the cooked tripe and pigs' tails, bacon, parsley, thyme, garlic, the remaining spring onions, bay leaf and cloves. Season with salt and pepper and add the whole chilli. Reduce the heat, add cold water to cover, put the lid on the pot and cook for 30 minutes over a low heat.

Add the *dombrés*, stir carefully but don't pierce the chilli. Add a little boiling water if necessary, to cover the *dombrés*, and cook for 20 minutes until the sauce is thick. Taste and add more salt if necessary. Remove the chilli. Serve hot.

CHICKEN FRICASSÉE

This is a go-to recipe. It's easy to make, with simple ingredients, and it requires minimal attention. Sometimes I replace the whole chicken with chicken legs and slow-cook for an additional 30 minutes until it falls off the bone. I then shred the meat and use it to stuff a *bokit*, instead of corned beef (p.64). Once it's cooked I slice it open and add a slice of tomato and some iceberg lettuce – and that's it, a chicken *bokit*.

Serves 4

1 whole chicken, cut into
    eight pieces
3 tbsp sunflower oil
juice of 2 limes
3 sprigs thyme
3 garlic cloves, crushed
1 tsp ground allspice
1 tsp mixed spice
salt and freshly ground black
    pepper
1 onion, chopped
2 spring onions (scallions),
    chopped
2 bay leaves
1 chicken stock (bouillon) cube,
    crumbled
1 tbsp golden granulated sugar
125ml/4fl oz/½ cup water
1 Scotch bonnet chilli

Marinate the chicken in the refrigerator overnight with 1 tablespoon of the oil, the lime juice, thyme, 1 garlic clove, allspice, mixed spice, salt and pepper.

Remove the chicken from the marinade (reserve the marinade) and pat dry with paper towels. Heat the remaining 2 tablespoons oil in a large heavy pot over a medium–high heat, add the chicken and cook, turning occasionally, until golden brown all over.

Add the onion, spring onions and the remaining garlic and cook for 2–3 minutes, until lightly browned.

Add the reserved marinade, bay leaves, stock cube and sugar, then add the water and the whole chilli, cover and cook over a low heat for 50 minutes.

Add another 4 tablespoons water and salt and pepper to taste. Stir, taking care not to burst the chilli, cover and cook for another 15 minutes.

Remove the chilli. Serve with boiled rice and stewed red kidney beans (p.128).

CREOLE CASSOULET

This recipe is a Creole version of the famous French cassoulet. It's slow-cooked; it's deliciously sweet from the carrots, with heaps of different flavours. It's not sexy on the plate, but guests never fail to ask for more. It's a crowd-pleaser, especially if you don't explain in detail what the ingredients are before you start eating. (Of course you'd say it's pork, but just not which part.) My most popular recipe yet!

Serves 4–6

2 salted pigs' tails
250g/9oz boneless pork loin, cut into 2–3cm/about 1in thick slices
4 tbsp sunflower oil
150g/5½oz smoked bacon slab, diced
1 can or vacuum pack (about 350g/12oz) frankfurters, drained
2 onions, chopped
4 garlic cloves, chopped
2 x 400g/14oz cans mixed peas and beans, drained and rinsed
3 sprigs parsley, chopped
2 sprigs thyme
3 carrots, sliced 2–3cm/about 1in thick
1 x 200g can or tube tomato purée (paste)
1 Scotch bonnet chilli
salt and freshly ground black pepper

Clean the pigs' tails in cold water, then put them in a saucepan, add cold water to cover, bring to the boil and boil for 20 minutes. Drain the pigs' tails and cut into pieces through the joints. Set aside. Cut each slice of pork loin into three pieces.

Heat half the oil in a frying pan (skillet) over a medium–high heat. Add the pork, bacon and sausages and brown all over. Set aside.

Heat the remaining oil in an ovenproof pot (Dutch oven) over a medium heat, add the onions and garlic and cook for 3–4 minutes. Add the mixed peas and beans. Add cold water to cover and add the parsley, thyme, carrots, tomato purée, the whole chilli, salt and pepper. Bring to simmering point, then cover with a well-fitting lid and simmer for 1½ hours, checking the level of water regularly and topping up if necessary to ensure it doesn't dry out.

Add all the meat and simmer for another 1½ hours.

Preheat the oven to 200°C/400°F/gas mark 6.

Taste the cassoulet and adjust the seasoning if necessary. Put the pot in the oven for 1 hour. Serve hot.

POULET AU CHATROU

OCTOPUS CHICKEN

The original recipe is for chicken and conch, but conch is virtually impossible to get in the UK unless you smuggle it in from France. I love octopus, so I've adapted the recipe. A Creole-style 'surf and turf', which I enjoy with boiled basmati rice.

Serves 4

1 large chicken, cut into eight
   pieces
juice of 2 limes
3 garlic cloves, crushed
salt and freshly ground black
   pepper
4 tbsp vegetable oil
1½ onions, very finely chopped
2 sprigs thyme
1 pinch ground allspice
4 sprigs parsley, finely chopped
100ml/3½fl oz/scant ½ cup water
2 bay leaves
1 Scotch bonnet chilli
500g/1lb 2oz octopus, gutted,
   cleaned and beak removed
2 spring onions (scallions), very
   finely chopped
2 tomatoes, chopped
2 heaped tbsp tomato purée
   (paste)

Marinate the chicken with the juice of 1 lime, 1 garlic clove, salt and pepper for at least 2 hours.

Remove the chicken from the marinade (discard the marinade) and pat dry with paper towels. Heat half the oil in a large heavy pot over a medium–high heat, add the chicken and cook for about 5 minutes, turning the pieces until golden brown all over.

Add 1 onion, 1 garlic clove, 1 thyme sprig, the allspice and half the parsley and cook for 2 minutes. Add the water, bay leaves, the whole chilli, salt and pepper and cook over a medium–low heat for 20 minutes.

Wash the octopus at least twice under fresh water and then clean it by rubbing it all over with the juice of a lime. Wrap the octopus in clingfilm (plastic wrap) and pound it with a mallet or a rolling pin (or the bottom of a heavy saucepan) for about 5 minutes.

Cut the octopus into small pieces. Heat the remaining oil in a saucepan over a medium heat and sauté the octopus with the remaining ½ onion and the spring onions, the remaining garlic, thyme, parsley, tomatoes and tomato purée, for about 8–10 minutes. Add salt and pepper to taste, then add the octopus to the chicken.

If you are using an ovenproof pot (Dutch oven), place it in the oven – preheated to 180°C/350°F/gas mark 4 – for 15–20 minutes. Alternatively, cover the pot with a well-fitting lid and simmer over a low heat for 35 minutes. Serve hot.

AILES DE DINDE BOUCANÉES

BUCCANEER TURKEY WINGS

Roadside food at its best. Buccaneer chicken is the most widespread version, but the same technique is applied to turkey wings and spare ribs. When on the way to the beach, this is the type of food you'd pick and enjoy with Creole rice (p.112) and your feet in the sand (and some *sauce chien* or hot creole sauce on the side). When we stop, everybody knows what I want: get me three turkey wings with a lot of sauce and I'm happy!

Serves 4

4 turkey wings
1 habanero chilli, very finely chopped
juice of 4 limes
1 tbsp sunflower oil
1 tbsp white vinegar
1 pinch ground cloves
salt and freshly ground black pepper
1 piece of sugar cane (with its skin on), about 90cm/3 feet long, cut into two or three to fit the barbecue

Make two cuts on each wing and marinate them in the refrigerator overnight with the chilli, lime juice, oil, vinegar, cloves, salt and pepper.

Light your barbecue charcoal and wait until the embers are white-hot. Put the sugar cane on the barbecue; it will produce thick smoke. Place the wings right where the smoke is thickest and cover the wings with foil or a stainless steel bowl. Grill for 45–50 minutes.

Alternatively, if you can't barbecue, cook the wings in a preheated oven at 220°C/425°F/gas mark 7 for 45–50 minutes; they won't have the smoky flavour but the marinade will do the trick.

TIP

If you're not a turkey person, replace with a whole chicken, cut into four joints.

GIGOT DE PÂQUES

EASTER SUNDAY LAMB

Just as in France, Creoles like to have lamb for Easter Sunday. It's usually served with yam gratin (p.122) and it needs to be well done.

Serves 6

1.5kg/3lb 5oz leg of lamb
salt and freshly ground black
   pepper
3 tbsp sunflower oil
juice of 2 limes
1 Scotch bonnet chilli, chopped
1 onion, chopped
3 spring onions (scallions),
   chopped
6 sprigs thyme
2 tbsp Colombo powder (p.86)
1 tsp ground allspice
1 tsp mixed spice
8 garlic cloves, each chopped
   into 4
6 cloves, chopped in half
150ml/5fl oz/⅔ cup water

You will need to marinate the lamb overnight, or for at least 4 hours. Put the lamb in a large bowl or container with a lid: it must be big enough to contain the lamb and small enough to fit in the refrigerator. Rub the leg with salt, pepper, 1 tablespoon of the oil and the lime juice. Wearing rubber gloves, rub the leg all over with the chopped chilli, onion, spring onions and thyme. Sprinkle the Colombo powder, allspice and mixed spice all over the lamb. Using a small sharp knife, stab the leg all over and insert the pieces of garlic and the cloves into the holes. Drizzle with another tablespoon of oil, cover and leave to marinate.

Preheat the oven to 200°C/400°F/gas mark 6.

Put the lamb in a roasting pan, reserving the marinade. Drizzle the remaining oil over the lamb. Put the lamb in the oven. Every 15 minutes, turn the lamb to ensure it cooks evenly; stir the jus in the roasting pan and spoon over the leg every time you turn it. After about 40 minutes, remove the lamb from the oven, baste with the reserved marinade and add the water. Return to the oven and cook for another 35–40 minutes (about 75 minutes in total).

When the lamb is cooked to your liking (see Tip), remove from the oven, cover with foil and leave to rest for 10–15 minutes before carving and serving.

Strain the sauce through a fine sieve and, if necessary, boil to reduce and thicken slightly before serving with the lamb.

TIP

In Creole food, meat is very well cooked. If you like your lamb a bit pink, cook it for 60 minutes, but use a meat thermometer to check the internal temperature, which should be 55°–60°C.

BREADFRUIT AND PORK PARMENTIER

Tout est bon dans le cochon ('in the pig, everything is good') is more than just a French saying. The best way to pay tribute to the animal to use it fully. This is one way to do so.

Serves 4

1kg/2lb 4oz boneless pork shoulder
salt and freshly ground black pepper
½ tsp mixed spice
½ tsp ground allspice
1 tbsp Colombo powder (p.86)
6 garlic cloves, crushed
1 Scotch bonnet chilli, finely chopped
2 onions, very finely chopped
2 Maggi cubes, dissolved in 300ml/10fl oz/1¼ cups boiling water
1 breadfruit
50g/1¾oz/4 tbsp butter, plus extra for topping
200ml/7fl oz/scant 1 cup milk
1 tbsp crème fraîche
100g/3½oz Emmental cheese, grated
1 tbsp vegetable oil, plus 2 tbsp sunflower oil

TIP

You can reserve the sauce and use it to cook vegetables.

Preheat the oven to 180°C/350°F/gas mark 4.

Cut off any excess fat from the shoulder. Sprinkle the pork with salt, pepper, mixed spice, allspice and Colombo powder and rub them in. Using a small sharp knife, pierce the shoulder all over and push the garlic and chilli into the holes.

Put the pork in an ovenproof pot (Dutch oven). Add the onions. Pour the Maggi stock over the pork: it should come about halfway up the pork. Cover the pot with a well-fitting lid and place it in the oven for about 2 hours.

Peel the breadfruit, cut into quarters and cut out the core. Place in a pan of lightly salted boiling water and boil for 40 minutes. Drain the water and mash with a fork. Add the butter, milk and crème fraîche. Mix well, taste and add more salt if necessary.

Check the pork: if it is fork tender and falling apart, remove it from the oven. If not, cook it for another 30 minutes.

Remove the pot from the oven, take the pork out of the sauce and place in a large dish. Shred the meat with a fork and knife.

Spread half of the breadfruit purée in a large gratin dish. Cover with the pork and then with the rest of the purée. Sprinkle the cheese and a few knobs of butter over the surface and bake in the oven for 15 minutes, until the top is golden. Serve hot.

CREOLE BEEF POT ROAST

The best beef ragout I ever had was at my friend's grandmother's house. It cooked for hours in her tiny, very simple kitchen. It was salty, the cuts of beef were fatty with some bones, and the seasoning was to die for. She has since passed away, but from my delicious memories I have been able to replicate the recipe.

Serves 4

1.5kg/3lb 5oz stewing beef with
   bones and fat
5 garlic cloves: 2 crushed,
   3 very finely chopped
2 sprigs thyme
4 tbsp vegetable oil
juice of 1 lime
salt and freshly ground black
   pepper
2 onions, very finely chopped
1 tbsp ground allspice
1 tbsp mixed spice
2 bay leaves
1 tbsp white vinegar
1 Maggi cube
1 carrot, diced
1 Caribbean red habanero chilli
   (be extremely cautious)

Marinate the meat in the refrigerator overnight with 2 crushed garlic cloves, 1 sprig of thyme, 1 tablespoon oil, the lime juice, salt and pepper.

Remove the meat from the marinade and pat dry with paper towels. Heat the remaining oil in a large heavy pot over a medium-high heat, add the meat and brown well all over.

Add the onions and the remaining garlic and cook over a medium heat until softened. Add the remaining thyme, the allspice, mixed spice, bay leaves and the vinegar and stir. Add just enough hot water to cover the meat and add the Maggi cube, salt and pepper, the carrot and the whole chilli. Cover and cook over a very low heat for at least 2 hours.

Stir carefully to avoid piercing the chilli. The meat should be very tender; if not, cover and simmer for another 10–15 minutes. You may need to add a tiny bit more hot water.

Taste and adjust the seasoning and remove the chilli. Serve hot with Creole rice (p.112).

AKONPAYMAN

SIDES

◆◆◆◆◆◆◆◆◆

Creole food is all about feasting and indulging. If you stay true
to its roots you will find rich, delicious recipes that feed not
only your body but also your soul. Sides are sometimes as rich
as mains. A Creole plate is a full plate and if you eat in a Creole
household, you'd better not disappoint the cook by eating like
a bird. We want to feed you and leave you with a full tummy.
That's the Creole way!

CREOLE RICE

Creole rice (also called *riz melangé*) is a housewife's godsend. When she serves this rice — to which you can add chicken or fish — it means she was either in a rush, or just used whatever was in her cupboard. It's also a favourite to bring when spending a day on the beach with the family and barbecuing some chicken wings in situ.

Serves 4

2 eggs
2 tbsp vegetable oil
1 onion, very finely chopped
1 spring onion, very finely chopped
4 garlic cloves, very finely chopped
½ tsp Colombo powder (p.86)
½ tsp tomato purée (paste)
500g/1lb 2oz/2½ cups jasmine rice
1 can (about 300g/10½oz)
    sweetcorn, drained
500ml/18fl oz/2 cups water
2 chicken stock cubes
1 bay leaf
salt and freshly ground black
    pepper

Put the eggs in a saucepan of cold water, bring to simmering point and simmer for 7–10 minutes. Drain and rinse in cold water. Set aside.

Heat the oil in a large saucepan, add the onion, spring onion, garlic, Colombo powder and tomato purée and cook until the onions start to soften.

Add the rice and corn. Stir to coat the rice. Add the water, chicken cubes and bay leaf and stir well. Add salt and pepper. Cover and cook over a low heat for 25 minutes, stirring two or three times to ensure the rice doesn't stick to the bottom of the pan.

Cut each egg into six and stir into the rice. Remove the bay leaf and serve hot, for example with chicken fricassée (p.100).

RIZ AU GOMBOS

OKRA RICE

Okra was brought to the Caribbean on the slave boats. You'll find a similar recipe in African cuisine. It looks fabulous on the plate with something as simple as stewed chicken.

Serves 4

250g/9oz fresh okra
1 litre/1¾ pints/4 cups water
1 onion, very finely chopped
4 garlic cloves, very finely chopped
1 bay leaf
1 tbsp vegetable oil
salt and freshly ground black
    pepper
200ml/7fl oz/scant 1 cup coconut
    milk
600g/1lb 5oz/3¼ cups basmati rice

Slice the okra into 1cm/½in thick rings. Put them in a pot and add the water, onion, garlic, bay leaf, oil, salt and pepper. Bring to simmering point, then add the coconut milk and simmer for about 2 minutes.

Meanwhile, rinse the rice three times. Add the rice to the pot. Cover and cook over a low heat for about 25 minutes; stir after 10–12 minutes to ensure the okra is evenly distributed in the rice and is not sticking to the bottom of the pot. When the rice is cooked and has absorbed most of the liquid, but is still quite wet, it is ready to serve.

RIZ AU COCO

COCONUT RICE

A classic alternative to plain white rice, works well with a good old Colombo curry.

Serves 4

500g/1lb 2oz/2½ cups basmati rice
400ml/14fl oz/1⅔ cups coconut
    milk
3 tbsp water
salt
1 tbsp vegetable oil

Wash the rice in a mixing bowl at least three times, until the water is clear. Put the rice in a saucepan and add the coconut milk, water, salt and oil. Cover and cook over a low heat for 25 minutes; stir after 10–12 minutes to unstick rice from the bottom of the pan. Serve hot.

CINDY'S PLANTAIN GRATIN

My sister likes everything fried. She's greedy. Whatever you cook for her, if there's not butter or frying involved, she'll quickly go and fix it. I created this recipe for her because she loves bacon and it's a pleasure to see her face when she enjoys food. Makes my day!

Serves 4

2 plantains
4 tbsp sunflower oil
1 handful smoked lardons
30g/1oz/2 tbsp butter
45g/1½oz/5 tbsp plain (all-purpose) flour
500ml/18fl oz/2 cups milk
salt and freshly ground black pepper
1 pinch grated nutmeg
100g/3½oz Emmental cheese, grated

Preheat the oven to 200°C/400°F/gas mark 6.

Peel the plantains and slice them about 2cm/¾in thick.

Heat the oil in a frying pan (skillet) and fry the lardons until crisp. Add the plantains and cook for 2–3 minutes. Tip them into a gratin dish.

Make a béchamel sauce: melt the butter in a saucepan over a medium heat, add the flour and whisk thoroughly. Gradually add the milk, whisking until it thickens, then stir in salt, pepper, nutmeg and 20g/¾oz of the cheese.

Pour the béchamel over the plantains and sprinkle the remaining cheese over the top. Bake for 15 minutes, until golden. Serve hot.

MAMOUNE'S PLANTAIN GRATIN

My mother was the master of gratins, effortlessly whipping up these things to go with our Sunday lunch. She cooks Creole food faster than anyone else I've seen. She loves a good rich béchamel, with loads of cheese, so this dish is for her.

Serves 4

3 plantains
salt and freshly ground black
   pepper
30g/1oz/2 tbsp butter
45g/1½oz/5 tbsp plain (all-purpose)
   flour
500ml/18fl oz/2 cups milk
1 pinch grated nutmeg
200g/7oz Emmental cheese, grated

Preheat the oven to 200°C/400°F/gas mark 6.

Chop off the ends of the plantains and cut them in half. Place them in a pan of boiling water, add 2 pinches of salt and boil for 10 minutes. Drain the plantains and remove the skin, which should fall off quite easily. Slice the plantains about 3cm/1in thick.

Make a béchamel sauce: melt the butter in a saucepan over a medium heat, add the flour and whisk thoroughly. Gradually add the milk, whisking until it thickens, then stir in salt, pepper, nutmeg and 50g/1¾oz of the cheese.

Put a layer of plantains in a gratin dish, sprinkle some cheese over them, then add a layer of béchamel sauce. Repeat the layers. Sprinkle the remaining cheese over the top. Bake for 15 minutes, until golden. Serve hot.

RICE AND BEANS

In Guadeloupe and Martinique, kidney beans are either stewed (p.168) or cooked with rice, as here. This is a very easy recipe that's seen on every table.

Serves 4

200g/7oz dried red kidney beans
1.5 litres/2½ pints/1.5 quarts water
salt and freshly ground black
  pepper
1 bay leaf
1 clove
1 sprig thyme
200g/7oz smoked bacon slab,
  roughly chopped
1 large onion, chopped
2 garlic cloves, crushed
300g/10½oz/generous 1½ cups
  long-grain rice
3 tbsp sunflower oil
1 sprig parsley, finely chopped

Soak the kidney beans overnight.

Rinse the beans under running water. Put the beans in a pot with the water, a pinch of salt, the bay leaf, clove and thyme. Cover and cook over a medium heat for 2 hours.

Add the bacon and onion and cook for 30 minutes.

Meanwhile, rinse the rice three times, drain and set aside. When the beans are soft, add the rice and enough hot water to cover the rice by about 3cm/1in. Add the oil, salt and pepper, cover with the lid and simmer for 15 minutes, stirring regularly so nothing sticks to the bottom. When the rice is cooked and has absorbed the liquid, but is still moist, it is ready. Sprinkle with the parsley and serve.

GREEN BANANA CAKES

This is very close to what Haitians call banana *pézé*. I created this recipe in London after trying my friend's speciality; her mother is from Haiti. There's a massive Haitian community in Guadeloupe, primarily because extreme poverty drives many to migrate to find work and if they stay long enough they have a chance to obtain French nationality, social security and education for their family. It adds to the fusion and is what makes the Caribbean so beautiful. I love green bananas because of their dryness and simplicity. This is my humble take on the Haitian dish.

Serves 4

750g/1lb 10oz green bananas
3 tbsp vegetable oil, plus extra for your hands
4 garlic cloves, finely grated
1 spring onion (scallion), very finely chopped
1 egg, beaten
20g/¾oz/2½ tbsp plain (all-purpose) flour
salt and freshly ground black pepper

Coat your hands in oil to prevent the bananas from staining them. Peel the bananas, then coarsely grate them into a mixing bowl.

Add the garlic and spring onion, mix them together and then stir in the egg. Add the flour and stir to combine thoroughly, then season with salt and pepper to taste.

Heat the oil in a frying pan (skillet) over a medium heat. Drop three or four tablespoonfuls of the mixture into the frying pan and flatten them, then fry, turning once, until golden on both sides. Drain on paper towels. Repeat until you have used all the mixture. Serve hot.

GRATIN D'IGNAME

YAM GRATIN

If you're having Easter lamb roast in Guadeloupe or Martinique, nine times out of ten it will be served with yam gratin. It's just one of those things. Try this one and serve it with lamb.

Serves 4–6

1kg/2lb 4oz yam
salt and freshly ground black
  pepper
2 tbsp sunflower oil
1 onion, very finely chopped
1 spring onion (scallion),
  very finely chopped
2 sprigs parsley, very finely
  chopped
1 tbsp cornflour (cornstarch)
350ml/12fl oz/1½ cups milk
100g/3½oz Emmental cheese,
  grated

Preheat the oven to 180°C/350°F/gas mark 4.

Peel the yam and cut into small chunks. Place in a pan of lightly salted boiling water and boil for 30 minutes, until tender. Drain and mash with a fork. Set aside.

Heat the oil in a saucepan, add the onion, spring onion and parsley and sauté for 2 minutes. Add the cornflour and stir, then gradually add the milk, stirring all the time until smooth. Add some pepper and a third of the cheese. Stir into the mashed yam, and add salt and pepper to taste.

Transfer the mash to a gratin dish. Sprinkle the remaining cheese over the top. Bake for 30 minutes, until golden, patched with brown. Serve hot.

GREEN PAPAYA GRATIN

This is a classic of Creole Caribbean cuisine. If you can't find green papayas, choose the least ripe of those you find. When ripe, the papayas have a bit of sweetness that will be enjoyable anyway.

Serves 4

1.5kg/3lb 5oz green papayas
salt and freshly ground black
    pepper
2 tbsp sunflower oil
50g/1¾oz/4 tbsp butter
2 garlic cloves, finely chopped
3 spring onions (scallions), sliced
2 tbsp chopped parsley
500ml/18fl oz/2 cups milk
150g/5½oz Gruyère cheese, grated,
    plus extra for sprinkling

Preheat the oven to 220°C/425°F/gas mark 7.

Cut the papayas in half, peel and scoop out the seeds. Cook them in salted boiling water for about 20 minutes (10 minutes if using ripe papayas), then drain and mash with a fork.

Heat the oil and butter in a saucepan over a medium–low heat. Add the garlic and spring onions and cook for 2 minutes. Stir in the parsley. Add the milk, the mashed papaya and the cheese. Stir and remove from the heat.

Divide this mixture among four ramekins. Sprinkle with grated cheese. Bake for 10 minutes, until golden. Serve hot with chicken or octopus fricassée (p.138 or p.107).

FRIED OKRA

This simple classic Creole Caribbean dish was very popular when I was growing up, but the tradition of making it seems to have disappeared. It's an indispensable recipe in the repertoire of any Creole cook.

Serves 4

250g/9oz fresh okra
1 egg
1 tbsp coconut milk
1 tbsp ground allspice
1 tbsp Colombo powder (p.41)
1 tsp hot chilli powder
salt and freshly ground black
    pepper
50g/1¾oz/7 tbsp plain (all-purpose)
    flour
250ml/9fl oz/1 cup vegetable oil

Wash the okra thoroughly.

Whisk the egg and coconut milk together until completely smooth. Dip the okra in the egg mixture, then place in a mixing bowl. Sprinkle over the allspice, Colombo powder, chilli powder, salt and pepper and toss gently to coat evenly. Add the flour and stir to coat evenly.

Heat the oil in a frying pan (skillet) over a medium heat until it reaches 180°C/350°F, or until a cube of bread browns in 3 seconds. Gently drop the okra into the oil and cook for 4–5 minutes, turning occasionally, until golden and crisp.

Using a slotted spoon, scoop the okra out of the oil and drain on paper towels. Serve hot, with *sauce chien* (p.190) on the side if you like.

STEWED LENTILS

Good things come to those who wait. When my dad was making these I remember going back and forth, lifting the lid to check whether they were ready. It takes ages – you can watch a movie while these are simmering – but the flavours are worth it in the end.

Serves 4

250g/9oz/1¼ cups green or brown lentils
2 tbsp sunflower oil
1 onion, roughly chopped
2 spring onions (scallions), chopped
3 garlic cloves, roughly crushed
500ml/18floz/2 cups hot water
1 salted pig's tail (optional)
200g/7oz smoked bacon slab, cut into chunks
1 carrot, diced
2 sprigs thyme
1 clove
1 bay leaf
1 large slice (about 400g/14oz) of calabaza (West Indian pumpkin), peeled and cubed
salt and freshly ground black pepper
2 sprigs parsley

Soak the lentils overnight in a covered bowl.

Rinse the lentils in two changes of cold water and drain in a colander.

Heat the oil in a pot over a medium heat and sauté the onion, spring onions and garlic. Add the lentils and cover with the hot water. Simmer, covered, for 35 minutes.

Meanwhile, clean the pig's tail in cold water, then put it in a saucepan, add cold water to cover, bring to the boil and boil for 20 minutes. Drain and cut into pieces through the joints.

Add the pig's tail and bacon to the lentils, together with the carrot, thyme, clove and bay leaf and cook, covered, over a medium–low heat for 30 minutes.

Add the calabaza. If the lentils are drying out, add a few tablespoons of water. Taste and adjust the seasoning. Add the parsley, cover and simmer for another 30 minutes, until thick.

Serve hot with salt cod brandade (p.87) or with fried fish and rice.

TIP

If using canned lentils, halve all the lentil cooking times.

STEWED RED KIDNEY BEANS

Almost everyone in Guadeloupe and Martinique has a pressure cooker, which means that this dish can be made in a third of the time. I don't have a pressure cooker in London, so patience is key, as this takes 3 hours of slow cooking. This stew is as traditional as it gets: it's on Creole tables every week, at least on Sundays, without exception.

Serves 4

400g/14oz dried red kidney beans
2 tbsp vegetable oil
1 onion, sliced
2 spring onions (scallions), sliced
3 garlic cloves, crushed
2 sprigs thyme
1 bay leaf
1 clove
200g/7oz smoked bacon slab,
   roughly chopped
900ml/1½pints/3¾ cups hot water
salt and freshly ground black
   pepper
2 sprigs parsley, chopped

Soak the kidney beans overnight.

Drain the beans and rinse in a colander.

Heat the oil in a large pot over a medium heat, add the onion and spring onions and cook until the onions have softened. Add the beans and the garlic. Stir and cover with about 800ml/28fl oz/3⅓ cups hot water. Add the thyme, bay leaf and clove, cover and simmer over a low heat for 1 hour.

Add the bacon and the remaining water and cook, covered, for another hour.

Add salt and pepper to taste and cook for another 30–45 minutes, until the beans are coated in a thick sauce. Stir in the parsley and cook over a low heat for another 15 minutes. Serve alongside white rice, with a meat ragout.

TIP

If using canned beans divide
all cooking times by three.

IGNAME ET POIS DE BOIS

STEWED GREEN PIGEON PEAS AND YAM

When you cook this, it will smell like a Creole Christmas in your kitchen. It's traditionally served with the Creole pork ragout (p.92), but it's a festive recipe that can be cooked throughout the year to extend the holiday spirit.

Serves 4

2 tbsp vegetable oil
200g/7oz smoked bacon slab, cut into chunks
2 onions, chopped
6 spring onions (scallions), chopped
1 large slice (about 400g/14oz) of calabaza (West Indian pumpkin), peeled and cubed, or 2 carrots, peeled and chopped
3 garlic cloves, crushed
3–4 sprigs parsley, chopped
2–3 sprigs thyme, leaves only
500g/1lb 2oz canned green pigeon peas (gungo peas), drained and rinsed
1 tsp ground black pepper
6 cloves
3 bay leaves
1 small piece (200g/7oz) of yam (the size of a potato)
salt

Heat the oil in a pot over a medium heat and fry the bacon with the onions, spring onions, calabaza, garlic, parsley and thyme for about 5 minutes, stirring, until the bacon is golden brown all over.

Add the pigeon peas and cook for 15 minutes.

Add the pepper, cloves, bay leaves and the piece of yam. Cover with hot water, add a good pinch of salt and cook, covered, for 45 minutes.

Remove the lid and cook for an additional 10 minutes, to reduce and thicken the liquid.

Using a fork, crush the piece of yam against the wall of the pot. Remove the bay leaf and serve hot.

Serve at Christmas with pork ragout and boiled yams to follow tradition, or with rice and chicken fricassée at any time of year.

GIRAUMONADE

CALABAZA (PUMPKIN) MASH

A visit to my coffee-planting friends on the leeward coast of Guadeloupe changed my views on this dish. I had always thought of *giraumonade* as a way of disguising pumpkin, but my friends used a pumpkin they had grown themselves and made it the focus of the dish. They prepared it in the most rural, rustic way, in a basic tin-roofed hut, with an even more basic kitchen with next to no utensils. To this day, it's the best I have ever had.

Serves 4

1kg/2lb 4oz calabaza (West Indian pumpkin), peeled and cubed
salt and freshly ground black pepper
1 tbsp sunflower oil
100g/3½oz smoked lardons
3 spring onions (scallions), finely chopped
3 garlic cloves, crushed
1 sprig thyme, leaves only
2 sprigs parsley, chopped
1 knob of butter

Put the calabaza in a pan of boiling water with 2 pinches of salt and boil for 15–20 minutes, until very tender. Drain and mash with a fork.

Heat the oil in a saucepan, add the lardons and cook for about 2 minutes. Add the spring onions, garlic, thyme and parsley. Stir in the mashed calabaza and add a knob of butter. Taste and adjust the seasoning. Serve hot.

SOUPS

Creole tradition dictates you have soup at least one night a
week. It's very likely to be Sunday night after the feast enjoyed
for lunch. Some soups, such as fat soup, are the kind we have
every week. Others, such as *pâté en pot*, are celebration soups.
The sweet potato and ginger soup in this chapter is one
I developed when away from home on cold nights in Europe.

PÂTÉ EN POT

Pâté en pot is the soup of celebrations, christenings and weddings because it requires
meticulous work to prepare but results in such rich, authentic flavours. I admit
that mudgeon, ruffle and caul are difficult to find: you need to order them from a
knowledgeable butcher, or you can leave them out. (Beef or lamb offal are fine too.)

Serves 6

1 heart, about 150g/5½oz
400g/14oz tripe
300g/10½oz mudgeon, ruffle or
  caul (optional)
juice of 3 limes
4 onions: 1 sliced, 3 finely chopped
6 cloves
4 bay leaves
10 garlic cloves: 5 crushed,
  5 very finely chopped
salt and freshly ground black
  pepper
5 tbsp vegetable oil
4 spring onions (scallions), very
  finely chopped
6 sprigs thyme
6 sprigs parsley, very finely
  chopped
3 carrots, very finely diced
2 parsnips, very finely diced
1 leek, very finely chopped
1 celery stalk, very finely diced
500g/1lb 2oz calabaza (West Indian
  pumpkin), very finely diced
2 pieces of yam (the size of small
  potatoes), very finely chopped
150g/5½oz smoked bacon slab,
  very finely diced
2 Maggi cubes or liquid seasoning
1 habanero chilli
1 small jar (100g/3½oz) capers,
  drained
500ml/18fl oz/2 cups dry white
  wine

Wash the offal under cold water and clean it thoroughly with the juice
of 3 limes. Put the offal in a large pot with the sliced onion, 3 cloves,
2 bay leaves, 5 crushed garlic cloves and 2 pinches of salt. Add cold
water to cover, bring to the boil over a low heat and simmer for 1 hour,
skimming regularly to remove the foam that appears on the surface.
When the offal is thoroughly cooked, drain, reserving the cooking
broth. Cut all the offal into very small cubes. Alternatively, if you can't
bear the meticulous work, chop the offal in a food processor until it
has a similar texture to a coarse mince.

Heat the oil in a large pot over a medium heat, add the finely chopped
onions, spring onions, thyme, parsley, and the remaining cloves and
finely chopped garlic. Cook for 2–3 minutes, until the onions have
softened.

Add the carrots, parsnips, leek, celery, pumpkin and yam. Stir, then add
the offal and bacon and stir thoroughly to ensure nothing sticks to the
bottom of the pot. Strain the offal broth and pour it over the meat and
vegetables. Add the cubes or liquid seasoning, salt and pepper and the
whole chilli. Cover with a lid and cook over a low heat for 1½ hours.

Add the wine and capers and cook for 15 minutes. Remove the chilli
and serve very hot.

CALABAZA AND PRAWN SOUP

In Guadeloupe and Martinique, calabaza grows like a weed. In my garden, they are huge: remember Cinderella's pumpkin coach, and you're getting the picture! One slice easily feeds four; leftover pumpkin freezes well.

Serves 4

1 large slice (about 500g/1lb 2oz) of calabaza (West Indian pumpkin), peeled and cubed
salt and freshly ground black pepper
1 onion, finely chopped
2 garlic cloves, crushed
2 sprigs parsley, chopped
250g/9oz raw peeled king prawns (large shrimp)
250ml/9fl oz/1 cup canned coconut milk
1 pinch grated nutmeg
30g/1oz/2 tbsp butter

Put the calabaza in a pan of boiling water with a pinch of salt and pepper, the onion, garlic, parsley and prawns and boil for 15 minutes, until the calabaza is tender.

Pour the contents of the pan into a food processor, add the coconut milk and nutmeg and blend until smooth, then return to the pan and cook over a low heat for 10 minutes.

Season with salt and pepper to taste, stir in the butter and serve hot.

SWEET POTATO AND GINGER CREAM SOUP

There are many types of sweet potatoes, but until I moved to Europe, I'd never seen an orange-fleshed potato. I think this recipe is best made with the purple-skinned, white-fleshed sweet potatoes – but the orange-fleshed variety works well too. This recipe combines the sweetness of the potato with a kick to shake the cold off your body.

Serves 4

30g/1oz/2 tbsp butter
500g/1lb 2oz sweet potatoes, peeled and cut into chunks
1 leek, sliced
2 garlic cloves, crushed
1 litre/1¾ pints/4 cups chicken stock
30g/1oz fresh ginger, peeled and grated
salt and freshly ground black pepper
4 tbsp crème fraîche

Melt the butter in a pot over a medium heat, add the sweet potatoes, leek and garlic and cook for about 8 minutes. Add the stock and cook for 15 minutes.

Add the ginger, salt and pepper and cook for 20 minutes.

Blend until smooth, then return to the pot and cook over a low heat for 5 minutes. Stir in the crème fraîche and serve hot.

COCONUT POTAGE

Everyone who knows me well knows I'm a sucker for coconuts. This is quite light and I can drink a whole pot of it on my own in a heartbeat. You really need to buy a coconut and make your own coconut milk for this soup.

Serves 2

1 coconut, milked (p.31)
500ml/18fl oz/2 cups vegetable
    stock
¼ Scotch bonnet chilli,
    very finely chopped
salt and freshly ground black
    pepper
1 pinch Colombo powder (p.86)
1 pinch grated nutmeg
2 sprigs parsley, finely chopped
200ml/7fl oz/scant 1 cup crème
    fraîche

Pour the coconut milk, stock and chilli into a large pot. Add salt and pepper, the Colombo powder and a pinch of nutmeg. Cook over a medium heat for 20 minutes.

Mix the parsley with the crème fraîche and stir it into the soup before serving.

TIP

You can make your own coconut milk by placing the fresh coconut flesh in a juicer, or blending it with 400ml/14fl oz/1 cups lukewarm water until completely puréed. You then strain the liquid through a tea towel or muslin (cheesecloth). Some supermarkets now sell chunks of fresh coconut, so you can make coconut milk without bashing a coconut husk. But if you're not feeling adventurous, canned coconut can of course be used instead.

CONGO SOUP

Most of the slaves that were brought to Guadeloupe and Martinique came from the Congo. Modern Creole still contains plenty of elements from the Bantu languages these slaves brought with them from Africa. This soup is a tribute to our history and is usually consumed during the rainy season.

Serves 6

400g/14oz salted beef
4 salted pigs' tails
1.5 litres/2½ pints/1½ quarts water
200g/7oz frozen green pigeon peas, or drained canned pigeon peas
200g/7oz frozen butter (lima) beans, or drained canned butter beans
200g/7oz frozen hyacinth beans (green Indian beans), or broad (fava) beans
2 tbsp sunflower oil
1 large yam (about 1.5kg/3lb 5oz), peeled and cut into chunks
1 large slice (about 250g/9oz) of calabaza (West Indian or any other pumpkin), peeled and cut into chunks
2 small malangas (eddo) or dasheen (taro), peeled and cut into chunks
3 white-fleshed sweet potatoes, peeled and cut into chunks
1 onion, chopped
5 garlic cloves, chopped
1 bouquet garni
3 cloves
salt and freshly ground black pepper

Rinse the salted beef and pigs' tails in cold water. Cut the meat into chunks and chop the pigs' tails into pieces through the joints. Put them in a pot, add the water, bring to the boil and boil for 20 minutes. Drain the meat, reserving the broth.

Meanwhile, if using frozen beans, put them in a bowl and cover with boiling water for a few minutes. Drain and rinse the beans.

Heat the oil in a pot and add the beans, all the vegetables, garlic, bouquet garni, the meat and its broth. Bring to the boil and boil for about 10 minutes, then cover and simmer for 1½ hours, or until the pigeon peas have burst and are tender. Serve hot.

SOUPE GRASSE

FAT SOUP

In Guadeloupe and Martinique, this is *the* Sunday evening soup. After a heavy Sunday lunch, we don't need another big meal. It's called fat soup because we love to use really fatty meats to make it. You invariably will have fat soup on a Sunday and, if you don't make it yourself, you'll go to someone's house and you're sure to come home with a bowl. It's a tradition. There are many ways of making this soup; this is my version.

Serves 4

3 tbsp vegetable oil
1kg/2lb 4oz pieces of braising beef
    and bony cuts, such as chuck,
    short rib, hock, oxtail, cow's foot,
    chopped into large chunks
1 onion, sliced
1 bay leaf
2 sprigs parsley
2 sprigs thyme
3 garlic cloves, crushed
salt and freshly ground black
    pepper
1.5 litres/2½ pints/1½ quarts water
3 carrots, diced
2 parsnips, diced
1 slice (150–200g/5–7oz) of
    calabaza (West Indian pumpkin),
    peeled and diced
2 leeks, diced
2 celery stalks, diced
¼ green cabbage, chopped
2 cloves
1 handful vermicelli pasta

Heat 2 tablespoons of the oil in a pot over a medium-high heat and brown the meat thoroughly all over.

Add the onion, bay leaf, parsley, thyme, garlic, salt and pepper and cover with the water. Bring to the boil over a low heat, skimming off the foam that appears on the surface.

Add all the vegetables and the cloves and simmer over a very low heat for 2–3 hours, skimming regularly to remove the foam.

Add the vermicelli, 1 tablespoon oil, salt and pepper and simmer for 20 minutes. Serve hot.

SAUCES AND CONDIMENTS

These sauces combine chillies and garlic with other flavours;
they are meant to take your food up a notch. You'll always
find at least one of them on a Creole table; if they are missing,
someone will be sure to ask for them.

SAUCE CHIEN

A sauce with a strange name. Some suggest it's because you can use it for everything – marinade, dip, dressing – and it follows you everywhere. In fact, it comes from the knife used to chop the ingredients: the *couteau chien* (a brand; 'dog knife').

Makes about 500g/1lb 2oz

1 onion, very finely chopped
2 spring onions (scallions), very finely chopped
2 garlic cloves, very finely chopped
1 habanero chilli, very finely chopped
1 tomato, very finely chopped
2 sprigs parsley, finely chopped
4 tbsp sunflower oil
juice of 1 lime
salt and freshly ground black pepper

Combine all the chopped ingredients in a bowl, then pour in the oil and lime juice. Season with salt and pepper to taste, mix well, then add 4 tablespoons hot water, stir and serve right away, or cover and keep in the refrigerator for 2 days.

SAUCE CREOLE

HOT CREOLE SAUCE

If you can really handle chilli, this is what you pour over your grilled meat and fish.

Makes about 375g/13oz

2 onions, roughly chopped
2 garlic cloves, peeled
1 habanero chilli
3 tbsp sunflower oil
juice of 1 lime
salt and freshly ground black pepper

Put the onion, garlic and the whole chilli in a food processor and blend for about 20 seconds. Pour in the oil and lime juice and blend for 10 seconds. Season with salt and pepper to taste. Pour into a jar and serve right away or cover and keep in the refrigerator for 2 days.

CRÈME D'AVOCAT

AVOCADO CREAM

This spread is amazing in a Creole-style bruschetta with smoked herring or saltfish _chiquetaille_ (p.58 or p.41). In a sandwich, as a dip, as a side, in your _bokit_ (p.64), the possibilities are endless.

Serves 4–6

2 large ripe green avocados
2 garlic cloves, crushed
1 sprig parsley, chopped
¼ habanero chilli, chopped
juice of 1 lime
salt and freshly ground black
   pepper

Cut the avocados in half and scoop out the flesh. Place in a food processor and add the garlic, parsley, chilli and lime juice. Blend until smooth. Season with salt and pepper to taste. Serve right away.

PRESERVED CHILLIES

There's always one person who can never have enough chilli. In my house, it's my mother.

**Makes about 2 x 400g/
14oz jars**

20 habanero chillies
salt and freshly ground black
     pepper
2 onions, roughly chopped
4 garlic cloves, crushed
5 bay leaves
10 cloves
5 sprigs thyme, roughly chopped
500ml/18fl oz/2 cups vegetable oil
500ml/18fl oz/2 cups white vinegar

Cut the chillies in half and put them into sterilized jars. Add salt and pepper, the onions, garlic, bay leaves, cloves and thyme. Pour in the oil and vinegar, and add a little more salt and pepper.

Macerate for at least a week before using. Keep in the refrigerator for up to 6 months. Always use a clean spoon to avoid contamination.

CHILLI PURÉE

A very fiery sauce. Serve in a small dish for those who want to give their dishes a kick.

Makes about 375g/13oz

12 habanero chillies
2 garlic cloves, peeled
1 onion, roughly chopped
1 Maggi cube
juice of 1 lime
1 tbsp vegetable oil

Blend the whole chillies, garlic, onion, Maggi cube and lime juice in a food processor until evenly mixed.

Heat the oil in a saucepan over a low heat and pour in the chilli purée. Cover and simmer for 3–4 minutes.

Leave to cool, then pour into a jar and place in the refrigerator for about 1 hour. Ideally, eat on the same day.

SYRUPS

These will make your cocktails and desserts taste heavenly.
If you are feeling daring, try them drizzled over salad leaves;
passion fruit and grenadine work especially well.

CANE SYRUP

Cane syrup is everywhere in Creole food. It's in cocktails, in desserts, and if you want to caramelize your meat you can add a few tablespoons of cane syrup. You basically have to have a bottle of this in your kitchen. Crucial!

Makes about 1 litre/1¾ pints/ 1 quart

1kg/2lb 4oz/5 cups golden granulated sugar
1.2 litres/2 pints/5 cups water
juice of 2 limes
2 pinches grated cinnamon
1 pinch grated nutmeg
1 vanilla pod, cut in half lengthwise

Put the sugar in a large saucepan and add the water. Add the lime juice, cinnamon, nutmeg and vanilla pod. Cook over a low heat for about 25 minutes, stirring continuously with a wooden spoon until the sugar has completely dissolved.

Remove the vanilla pod and leave to cool.

Using a funnel, pour the syrup into a sterilized bottle. Keep in the refrigerator for up to 2–3 months.

SORREL SYRUP

This is the basis of the Christmas punch. You use it to make a *ti' punch* (p.54), replacing the sugar or cane syrup with this bad boy. Festive flavours all the way!

Makes about 1.5 litres/2½ pints/1½ quarts

500g/1lb 2oz dried sorrel (hibiscus) petals – or 1kg/2lb 4oz fresh sorrel when in season
zest of 1 lime, peeled in strips, plus the juice
2 litres/3½ pints/2 quarts water
600g/1lb 5oz/3 cups golden granulated sugar
1 cinnamon stick
1 whole nutmeg, grated

If using fresh sorrel, soak the flowers in cold water with the juice of a lime for about 10 minutes. Drain the water. Peel the sorrel by discarding the core and keeping the petals.

Whether dried or fresh, place the petals in a large pot and cover with the water. Bring to the boil and boil for about 45 minutes. Strain, reserving the cooking water.

Put the sorrel water in a pot, add the sugar, cinnamon stick, nutmeg and lime zest and simmer for 1 hour.

Leave to cool, then pour into a sterilized large airtight jar or empty rum bottles. Keep in the refrigerator for up to a month.

TIP

This makes a thick syrup. If you want it to be a bit more runny, add about 500ml/18fl oz/ 2 cups more water when boiling the sorrel.

GRENADINE SYRUP

When I moved to England, it was difficult to find grenadine syrup, so I decided to make my own. Crucial for your planteur cocktail (p.30), it can also be drunk with ice and water/soda/lemonade, or poured over ice cream.

Makes about 300ml/10fl oz/ 1¼ cups

350ml/12fl oz/1½ cups 100% pure pomegranate juice
175g/6 oz/generous ¾ cup golden granulated sugar
juice of ½ lime

Put the pomegranate juice in a saucepan and bring to the boil. Add the sugar and lime juice and stir until the sugar has dissolved. Simmer for 45 minutes.

Leave to cool, then pour into a sterilized jar or an empty rum bottle. Keep in the refrigerator for 2–3 months.

SIROP DE MARACUDJA

PASSION FRUIT SYRUP

I love this syrup so much I often have it with cold water and ice with a lime wedge. When we were little, my brother and I would cut a passion fruit in half and share it. We'd pour in a tablespoon of cane syrup (p.154) and eat it with a teaspoon as a snack.

Makes about 300ml/10fl oz/ 1¼ cups

20 fresh passion fruits or 250ml/ 9fl oz/1 cup passion fruit juice
1 vanilla pod, cut in half lengthwise
150g/5½oz/¾ cup golden granulated sugar
juice of 1 lime
150ml/5fl oz/⅔ cup water

Cut the passion fruits in half and scoop the pulp into a saucepan. Using a small knife, scrape the seeds from the vanilla pod and add to the pan, together with the sugar, lime juice and water. Bring to a boil over a medium–high heat, stirring until the sugar has dissolved. Simmer for 10 minutes, until it becomes syrupy.

Leave to cool, then pour into a sterilized jar or an empty rum bottle. Keep in the refrigerator for up to a month.

DESSERTS

Creole food has so much to choose from when it comes to
sweet things. There's a huge array of tropical fruits and these
are often combined with French techniques to make desserts
you'd never dreamed of. Sometimes the simplest things make
the perfect finale for an exotic dinner; sometimes an impressive
cake is needed for a celebration. These are a few
of my favourite desserts.

BANANA AND RUM FRITTERS

Carnival equals sweet fritters. These treats are served every Sunday throughout January and until Ash Wednesday.

Makes about 20–30 fritters

4 ripe bananas
60g/2¼oz/5 tbsp golden granulated
    sugar
2 eggs
125g/4½oz/1 cup plain (all-
    purpose) flour
1 tsp baking powder
1 vanilla pod, cut in half lengthwise
grated zest of 1 lime
1 pinch grated cinnamon
1 pinch grated nutmeg
1 tbsp white rum
1 litre/1¾ pints/4 cups sunflower oil
1 tbsp icing (confectioners') sugar

Peel the bananas, put them in a bowl and mash with a fork. Whisk in the sugar and eggs, then the flour and baking powder. Using a small knife, scrape the seeds from the vanilla pod and add to the mixture, then stir in the lime zest, cinnamon, nutmeg and rum.

In a deep pan, heat the oil over a medium heat until it reaches 180°C/350°F, or until a cube of bread browns in 30–40 seconds. Make sure the oil doesn't get too hot and start to smoke. Gently drop tablespoonfuls of the batter into the oil and cook for about 2 minutes on each side, turning occasionally, until dark golden all over.

Scoop the fritters out of the oil and drain on paper towels. Sprinkle with icing sugar and serve hot.

TIP

I like to add a tablespoon of unsweetened desiccated (dry) coconut to my banana fritters to add texture.

LOVE TORMENT

This recipe is from Les Saintes, two small islands that form part of the archipelago of Guadeloupe.

Makes 6–8 cakes

600g/1lb 5oz shortcrust pastry
   dough

Coconut jam
2 coconuts, finely grated
   (approximately 300g/10½oz)
600g/1lb 5oz/3 cups golden
   granulated sugar
1 cinnamon stick
1 pinch grated nutmeg
grated zest of 1 lime
1 vanilla pod, cut in half lengthwise

Crème pâtissière
250ml/9fl oz/1 cup milk
50g/1¾oz/¼ cup caster (superfine)
   sugar
1 egg
2 tbsp cornflour (cornstarch)
2 tbsp rum
1 tsp grated cinnamon
½ tsp grated nutmeg
grated zest of 1 lime
½ vanilla pod

Sponge
4 eggs
200g/7oz/1 cup golden caster
   (superfine) sugar
200g/7oz/generous 1½ cups plain
   (all-purpose) flour
200g/7oz/¾ cup unsalted butter,
   melted
½ vanilla pod
1 pinch grated cinnamon
1 pinch grated nutmeg
1 tbsp rum

Make the coconut jam first. Put the grated coconut in a saucepan with the sugar, cinnamon stick, nutmeg and lime zest and pour over 500ml/18fl oz/2 cups water. Using a small knife, scrape the seeds from the vanilla pod into the mixture with the pod. Cover and cook over a medium–high heat, stirring until the sugar has dissolved and skimming to remove the foam. Cook for 10 minutes, until the jam has thickened then leave to cool.

Grease 6–8 deep fluted tartlet tins, about 10cm/4in in diameter. Roll out the pastry and line the tins. Prick the pastry all over with a fork. Spread a layer of coconut jam over the pastry and place in the fridge.

To make the crème pâtissière, bring the milk to the boil in a saucepan. In a mixing bowl, whisk the sugar and egg together until the mixture thickens slightly, then add the cornflour and whisk evenly. Whisk in the hot milk, then return the mixture to the pan and cook over a low heat, whisking continuously until it's thick and starts bubbling. Remove from the heat and add the rum, cinnamon, nutmeg and lime zest; scrape the seeds from the vanilla pod into the mixture. Leave to cool.

Preheat the oven to 180°C/350°F/gas mark 4.

To make the sponge, beat the eggs with the sugar until light and fluffy. Whisk in the flour. Whisking continuously, add the melted butter. Add the vanilla seeds, cinnamon, nutmeg and rum.

Remove tartlets from refrigerator and divide the crème pâtissière among them, spreading it in a thin layer that covers the jam completely. Add the sponge batter, but do not overfill, as the cake will swell up as it bakes. Bake for 60 minutes, until well risen and golden. Then leave to cool before removing from the tins.

MONT BLANC COCONUT CAKE

The génoise gives a light and airy feel that makes it taste like a coconut cloud.

Serves 6

Génoise sponge
butter for greasing
4 eggs, separated
1 pinch salt
125g/4½oz/1 cup plain (all-
   purpose) flour
1 tsp baking powder
125g/4½oz/generous ½ cup caster
   (superfine) sugar
2 pinches grated cinnamon
1 pinch grated nutmeg
1 tbsp rum

Coconut cream
400ml/14fl oz/1⅔ cups coconut
   milk
1 can (about 400g/14oz)
   condensed milk
2 tbsp cornflour (cornstarch)
100ml/3½fl oz/scant ½ cup water
1 tbsp rum
grated zest of 1 lime

To decorate
1 coconut
glacé cherries (optional)

Preheat the oven to 180°C/350°F/gas mark 4. Grease and line a 24cm/9½in round cake tin.

First make the sponge cake. In a mixing bowl, beat the egg whites with a pinch of salt until stiff peaks form. Sift the flour and baking powder into another mixing bowl. When the egg whites are stiff, add the sugar and carry on whisking. Once the mixture is firm, add the egg yolks, whisking continuously. Still whisking, add the flour and the spices and carry on whisking for another 2–3 minutes. Pour the batter into the prepared tin and place in the oven for 20–25 minutes, until well risen, with a nice golden top.

Remove the cake from the oven and leave to cool in its tin.

To make the coconut cream, pour the coconut milk, condensed milk, cornflour and water in a saucepan and simmer for a few minutes, stirring constantly, until thick and creamy. Add the rum and lime zest and leave to cool.

When the cake is cool, turn it out onto a piece of greaseproof (wax) paper. Slice it in half horizontally, with the cut sides facing up. Sprinkle some rum over the cut sides. Spread some of the coconut cream evenly over both sides, then sandwich them together. Spread the remaining coconut cream over the top of the cake and all around the sides.

To decorate, break open the coconut and scoop out the meat. Peel and discard the brown skin. Wash the coconut meat under cold water and then grate it finely. Sprinkle the coconut all over the cake until completely covered. Scatter glacé cherries on top, if wished. Place it in the refrigerator for at least 4 hours before serving.

FLAMBÉ BANANAS

The most popular dessert in Guadeloupe and Martinique. Traditionally made with ordinary bananas, but we found them too soft and so my mum made a firmer version, using ripe plantains. It became a family recipe. When my sister and I lived in Paris, I would make these when I missed home – and my sister couldn't get enough. When she makes them, she uses cane syrup (p.154) instead of sugar and adds vanilla.

Serves 4

2 very ripe plantains
50g/1¾oz/4 tbsp butter
1 pinch grated cinnamon
1 pinch grated nutmeg
150g/5½oz/¾ cup golden
   granulated sugar
juice of 1 lime
3–4 tbsp white rum

Peel the plantains and slice them in three lengthwise. Melt the butter in a frying pan (skillet) and fry the plantains on both sides, until golden.

Add the cinnamon, nutmeg, sugar and lime juice. Pour the rum into the pan and immediately – standing well back as the flames leap up – either tilt the pan slightly so it touches the flame (if you have a gas hob) or hold a match near to the pan (on an electric hob) to flambé the bananas. Serve immediately.

TIP

Grate a little lime zest over the bananas before serving, and serve with coconut or vanilla ice cream.

TARTE À LA BANANE

BANANA PIE

I re-explored this recipe at my supper club. There was something I didn't like about the way traditional banana pies were made back home; I realized it was because the bananas are often sliced too thinly, which makes them too soft and mushy. I like the texture of banana and wanted to feel it in the pie. This is my take on the traditional Creole banana pie.

Serves 6

about 300g/10½oz shortcrust
    pastry dough
butter for greasing
5 bananas
4 eggs
6 tbsp golden caster (superfine)
    sugar
1 vanilla pod, cut in half lengthwise
300ml/10fl oz/1¼ cups double
    (heavy) cream
1 pinch grated cinnamon
1 pinch grated nutmeg
1 tbsp rum

Preheat the oven to 200°C/400°F/gas mark 6. Grease a 22cm/8½in tart tin.

On a lightly floured work surface, roll out the pastry quite thin and line the tart tin. Prick the pastry all over with a fork.

Peel the bananas and cut into rings about 1cm/½in thick, then arrange in a circle, one or two layers deep, on the pastry.

In a mixing bowl, whisk together the eggs and sugar until the sugar has dissolved. Using a small knife, scrape the seeds from the vanilla pod and add to the mixture, together with the cream, cinnamon, nutmeg and rum. Pour the mixture over the bananas, then place the pie in the oven. After about 30 minutes, when the pie starts to become golden, reduce the heat to 180°C/350°F/gas mark 4 and continue to bake for another 30 minutes, until the filling is firm to the touch. Leave to cool slightly before serving.

GÂTEAU PISTACHE

PEANUT CAKE

I have a love affair with this cake. I probably made this cake a hundred times before successfully replicating the taste, but it was worth it. Not the easiest recipe but definitely a winner!

Serves 6

Génoise sponge
butter for greasing
4 eggs, separated
1 pinch salt
125g/4½oz/1 cup plain (all-purpose) flour
1 tsp baking powder
125g/4½oz/generous ½ cup golden caster (superfine) sugar
3 pinches grated cinnamon
2 pinches grated nutmeg
1 tsp vanilla extract

Peanut buttercream
200g/7oz roasted monkey nuts, shelled
75ml/2½fl oz/5 tbsp water
100g/3½oz/½ cup golden caster (superfine) sugar
2 tsp vanilla sugar
2 eggs
250g/9oz/2 cups butter, softened, cut into cubes

(method continues overleaf)

Preheat the oven to 180°C/350°F/gas mark 4. Grease and line a 24cm/9½in round cake tin.

First make the sponge cake. In a mixing bowl, beat the egg whites with a pinch of salt until stiff peaks form. Sift the flour and baking powder into another mixing bowl. When the egg whites are stiff, add the sugar and carry on whisking. Once the mixture is firm, add the egg yolks, whisking continuously. Still whisking, add the flour, 2 pinches of cinnamon and a pinch of nutmeg and carry on whisking for another 2–3 minutes. Pour the batter into the prepared tin and place in the oven for 20–25 minutes, until well risen, with a nice golden top.

Remove the cake from the oven and leave to cool in its tin.

Put the monkey nuts on a baking sheet and roast them in the oven for about 15 minutes, shaking the baking sheet regularly so they roast evenly. Cool.

When the cake is cool, turn it out onto a piece of greaseproof (wax) paper. Slice it in half horizontally. In a small bowl, mix the vanilla extract with a pinch of cinnamon and nutmeg and sprinkle over the cut sides of the cake.

For the peanut buttercream, heat the water, sugar and vanilla sugar in a saucepan until the sugar has dissolved, bring to the boil and boil until the syrup reaches 120°C/250°F – the soft ball stage (see Tip). Meanwhile, put the eggs in a mixing bowl and whisk lightly. Gradually pour the hot syrup into the eggs, whisking continuously until the mixture has cooled down and is thick and smooth. Beat in the cubes of

butter one by one until you have a smooth buttercream.

Place 70g/2½oz of the peanuts in a food processor and blend to a powder. Add the powder to the buttercream. Spread some of the buttercream evenly over the bottom cake layer, then sandwich together with the top layer. Spread the remaining buttercream over the top of the cake and all around the sides.

Place in the refrigerator for 30 minutes.

Put the remaining peanuts in the food processor and blitz briefly until the nuts are in chunky pieces. Remove the cake from the refrigerator and sprinkle the peanuts over the top and around the sides of the cake. Keep the cake in the refrigerator until ready to serve.

ANANAS AU VIN

WINE PINEAPPLE

This recipe was an afternoon treat when we were children. It's well known to all children who grew up in the French Caribbean. Yes, the recipe contains wine – but the excuse would be that, compared to rum, wine is not strong, so children can have it. Not a very good excuse, but I wasn't complaining.

Serves 4

1 pineapple
50g/1¾oz/¼ cup golden granulated sugar
500ml/18fl oz/2 cups red wine
2 pinches grated cinnamon
2 pinches grated nutmeg
1 tsp vanilla extract

Peel the pineapple. Cut it into quarters and remove the core. Cut the pineapple into chunks and place the pieces in a large bowl. Sprinkle the sugar over, then add the wine, spices and vanilla. Stir, then place in the refrigerator for at least 2 hours before serving.

PÂTE DE GOYAVE

GUAVA CHEESE (GUAVA PASTE)

One of the things I used to pack in my suitcase when I flew away from home back to Europe was guava cheese. It's always in my cupboard. It can simply be spread on toast, but it's very versatile (see Tip) and now that I make my own I often use it in baking.

Makes about 200g/7oz

1kg/2lb 4oz ripe pink-fleshed guava
about 500g/1lb 2oz/2½ cups
    golden granulated sugar
juice of ½ lime

Wash the guavas and cut them into four. Put them in a saucepan and add water to cover. Put the lid on and cook over a medium heat, stirring regularly, until they are soft and easily pierced.

Scoop out the guava flesh with a slotted spoon and blend in a food processor until you have a smooth purée.

Weigh the purée (you should have around 500g/1lb 2oz) and weigh out an equal amount of sugar. Put the purée and sugar into a clean saucepan. Add the lime juice. Simmer for about 25–30 minutes, until the mixture is thick enough to stay separated when stirred with a wooden spoon. Pour onto a greased baking sheet (for thin guava cheese) or into a cake tin if you prefer thicker cubes of paste.

Leave to cool completely, then cut into cubes.

TIP

It's very sweet but you can eat it on its own, just like I did as a child. You can also use it to glaze meat, bake with it (p.180), or serve it with (dairy) cheese.

PINEAPPLE UPSIDE-DOWN CAKE

What's more Caribbean than a pineapple upside-down cake? Many of my students tell me they have found it difficult to make the sponge in the past: it comes out too hard, undercooked, or too flat. This recipe turns upside-down cake around and will make it your go-to recipe for a naughty treat.

Serves 6

250g/9oz/1¼ cups golden caster (superfine) sugar
1 ripe, very sweet pineapple, peeled, cored and cut into slices about 1cm/½in thick (canned pineapple rings are fine – you will need a 400g/14oz can, drained)
4 eggs
200g/7oz/generous 1½ cups plain (all-purpose) flour
1 tsp baking powder
200g/7oz/generous ¾ cup unsalted butter, very soft, but not liquid
2 tbsp rum
1 pinch grated cinnamon
1 pinch grated nutmeg
1 tsp vanilla extract

Preheat the oven to 200°C/400°F/gas mark 6.

Put 50g/1¾oz/4 tablespoons of sugar and 1 tablespoon of water in a 24cm/9½in diameter cake tin and place in the oven until the sugar caramelizes. Arrange the pineapple slices in the caramel.

In a large mixing bowl, whisk the eggs until they are light and fluffy. Whisk in the remaining sugar. Add the flour, baking powder and butter and whisk until the batter is smooth. Add the rum, cinnamon, nutmeg and vanilla.

Pour the batter over the pineapples and place in the oven. Bake for 40 minutes, or until a skewer inserted into the centre of the cake comes out clean.

Remove from the oven and leave to cool in the tin.

To serve, place a large plate over the top of the cake tin, flip them upside down and lift off the cake tin.

COCONUT FLAN

Coconut flan is a traditional recipe in the Creole islands. My mother used to make it as a Sunday afternoon treat. She said the secret was in the timing and the bain-marie. If we were good, my sister, brother and I would get two ramekins each. Very sweet and delicious.

Serves 6–8

1 can (about 400g/14oz)
  condensed milk
1 can (about 400ml/14fl oz)
  evaporated milk
4 eggs, separated
1 pinch grated cinnamon
1 pinch grated nutmeg
finely grated zest of ½ lime,
  plus 1 tsp juice
400ml/14fl oz/1⅔ cups canned
  coconut milk
1 tbsp unsweetened desiccated
  (dry) coconut (optional)
60g/2¼oz/5 tbsp golden granulated
  sugar
100ml/3½fl oz/7 tbsp water

Preheat the oven to 180 °C/350°F/gas mark 4.

In a bowl, combine the condensed and evaporated milk and egg yolks and whisk together. Add the cinnamon, nutmeg and lime zest. Gradually whisk in the coconut milk. Add the desiccated coconut, if using.

In another bowl, beat the egg whites until stiff peaks form. Gently fold in the coconut mixture.

Heat the sugar, lime juice and water in a small heavy-based saucepan over a medium heat until it forms a deep brown caramel, and pour a little into each ramekin.

Put the ramekins in a deep ovenproof dish and pour in enough boiling water to reach halfway up the ramekins. Pour the coconut flan mixture into the ramekins and bake in the bain-marie for 35 minutes, until just set.

Leave to cool at room temperature, then put in the refrigerator for at least 2 hours before serving.

GUAVA PASTRY

When you go to the beach, swim, frolic in the sand, it makes you hungry. Very hungry. Fortunately there are always a few market ladies around to cater to your hunger in the Caribbean. Their stalls offer refreshing icy 'snowballs' and coconut sorbets but also a large display of cakes, tarts, pies and pastries. This guava pastry is a classic: if you see one of these stalls and they don't have it, they must have run out, no other reason!

Makes 8 pastries

250g/9oz 2 cups plain (all-purpose) flour
125g/4½oz/generous ½ cup unsalted butter, softened
30g/1oz/2 tbsp caster (superfine) sugar
1 tsp salt
200ml/7fl oz/scant 1 cup water
150g/5½oz guava cheese (paste) (p.225), or quince cheese
1 egg yolk, lightly beaten

Put the flour in a large mixing bowl and make a well in the centre. Add the butter, sugar, salt and water to the well. Mix and knead until you have a smooth ball of dough. Set aside for at least 2 hours.

Preheat the oven to 180°C/350°F/gas mark 4.

Roll out the dough until it's 2mm/⅟₁₆in thick. Cut out 16 rectangles, 10 x 5cm/4 x 2in. Place a 4–5cm/about 2in piece of guava cheese in the centre of eight of the pieces of dough and cover with the remaining dough. Crimp the edges together with a fork and make a small cut in the centre of each. Brush with egg yolk. Bake for 20 minutes, until deep golden brown. Leave to cool before serving.

TIP

Instead of guava cheese, you can use banana jam (p.182) or coconut jam (p.164).

BANANA PASTRY

I never knew why this pastry is called *jalousie* in Martinique; in Guadeloupe we just call it *tarte banane*. I've discovered that the classic French *jalousie* pastry is so called because the cuts in the top make it look like slatted blind called a *jalousie* (rather like a Venetian blind); I guess a jealous lover could spy through this type of blind. Whatever the story, I love eating it. You don't have to make rectangles; you can use round cutters instead – that's how this is made in Guadeloupe. You can also use guava cheese (p.175) or coconut jam (p.164) for a change.

Makes 4 pastries

300g/10½oz puff pastry dough
1 egg yolk, lightly beaten

Banana jam
300ml/10fl oz/1¼ cups water
300g/10½oz/1½ cups golden
   granulated sugar
juice of 1 lime
1 vanilla pod, cut in half lengthwise
2 ripe bananas
juice of 1 orange
1 tbsp rum

To make the banana jam, put the water, sugar, lime juice and vanilla pod in a saucepan over a low heat for about 8 minutes, until you have a light brown syrup.

Peel the bananas and cut into rings about 2cm/¾in thick. Add the bananas and orange juice to the syrup and simmer for 20 minutes, stirring regularly to avoid it burning or sticking too much. Add the rum. Leave to cool.

Preheat the oven to 180°C/350°F/gas mark 4.

On a lightly floured work surface, roll out the puff pastry to about 4mm/¼in thick.

Cut out eight squares, 10 x 10cm/4 x 4in. Place 1 tablespoon of banana jam in the centre of four of the squares; be careful not to put too much. Cover with another square and make two parallel cuts, about 5cm/2in long, in the top. Crimp the edges together with your fingers and brush with egg yolk. Bake for 30 minutes, or until golden brown. Leave to cool before serving.

GRATIN DE MANGUE

MANGO GRATIN

This is easy! Very easy. I had my three-, four- and seven-year-old nieces and nephew make this a few months ago. They were so happy when they realized they could cook. If you have nice colourful ramekins, this dessert will wow any guests. Why not chop some mint and sprinkle it over to finish?

Serves 4

2 mangoes
40g/1½oz/3 tbsp butter, plus extra for topping
75ml/2½fl oz/5tbsp aged rum
1 vanilla pod, cut in half lengthwise
400ml/14fl oz/1⅔ cups coconut milk
40g/1½oz/3 tbsp golden granulated sugar
grated zest of 1 lime

Preheat the oven to 220°C/425°F/gas mark 7.

Peel the mangoes and slice the flesh lengthwise. Melt the butter in a frying pan (skillet), add the mangoes, rum and the seeds scraped from the vanilla pod, and cook for 5–6 minutes, until the mango begins to soften.

Divide the pieces of mango among four ramekins, and dot with butter. Pour 100ml/3½fl oz/scant ½ cup of coconut milk into each ramekin and sprinkle with a quarter of the sugar and the lime zest.

Place in the hot oven for about 3 minutes. Leave to cool before serving.

GLOSSARY

Accras (also spelt acras, akras)
Small fritters, most commonly made with saltfish. Originally from West Africa and made with black-eyed peas or vegetables.

Achiote (known locally as *roucou*)
Red dried seeds from a tree native to the Caribbean and South America. Achiote is the most authentic spice on the islands as it was used by the Amerindians before the arrival of the Europeans. It's now mainly used to colour cooking oil to make Creole fish court bouillon (p.110), and to make red butter (*beurre rouge* or *bè rouj*), a red-orange, salty, spicy lard made with ground achiote seeds.

Aji dulce (also known as sweet habanero pepper)
The Spanish name means 'sweet chilli'. A member of the *Capsicum chinense* family, aji dulce has a similar aroma and flavour complex to that of the red habanero, but without the intense heat.

Bacon (known locally as *lard fumé*)
We use smoked bacon for flavour in many recipes, especially stews. It can be smoked fatback, smoked pork belly, thick-cut smoked streaky bacon, or thick smoked lardons. Polish shops usually sell a smoked bacon slab that works very well in Creole recipes.

Bakes
A type of fried dough bread from Trinidad.

Baton kako (also known as *bwa kako* in Martinique)
A stick of pure cocoa paste. Used to make hot chocolate and a crucial element of the *pain au beurre et chocolat* served at celebrations in Martinique. The best Martiniquais chocolate is made out of this pure cocoa that retains all the natural flavours, aromas and qualities of pure cocoa mass and cocoa butter.

Baton lélé (also known as *bois lélé, bwa lélé*)
A small stick with three or five branches at the end, often from the wood of cocoa trees, used to whisk or stir drinks and food. Small batons lélés are used to stir *ti' punch* and coconut punch, bigger ones are used a bit like a potato masher, to stir *giraumonade*, *calalou* or *migan*.

Beans and peas
Beans and peas mean the same thing in the Caribbean. Rice and peas is rice and beans. Widely used in Creole cuisine, each variety has a specific taste and – if you want to make an authentic dish – they cannot be substituted for one. They are usually available in both dried and canned forms.

Blaff
Fish, shellfish or meat poached in an aromatic broth of herbs and spices. Blaff is supposedly the sound the fish or meat makes when you drop it into the broth. See pp.104, 115 and 141.

Bokit
A ball of fried dough filled with anything from meat to fish, most commonly chicken and saltfish.

Boucan
From the Amerindian language it means to 'wood grill'. A type of fire on which Caribs smoked meat and fish. It also designates the hut in which they did the smoking. Rather than quick grilling, it implies slow cooking over charcoal.

Breadfruit

Round, with a rough green skin and a cream to yellow flesh, breadfruit is a member of the mulberry family. Very starchy, it can be boiled, fried, puréed, and roasted and so is like the potato of the Caribbean. Also available in cans.

Calabash

A round gourd mainly used as a utensil after its flesh has been removed. It is used for cups, bowls, spoons, to store spices, carry water, marinate fish – pretty much anything that needs a container.

Calabaza (also known as Caribbean or West Indian pumpkin, locally known as *giraumon*)

A Caribbean variety of very large pumpkin with bright orange flesh and very large seeds. Sold in slices at exotic markets. It's used in stews and soups and in a Creole recipe called *giraumonade* (p.131). Its cousin, butternut squash, can be substituted.

Calalou (also spelled calallou, callaloo)

A classic Caribbean soup that varies from one island to another. It's made with callaloo leaves (dasheen or taro leaves), also known as kale or Chinese spinach (easily replaced with fresh spinach leaves) and often contains okra and pork meats like snout, bacon slab and pigs' tails. In the French islands, crab is used.

Cassava (also known as manioc, yucca)

A tuber with rought dark brown skin that looks like a log. There are sweet and sour varieties; both are poisonous when raw. Cassava use is inherited from the Amerindians and is used to make flour for flatbreads and crepes, tapioca, and is also boiled and eaten as a vegetable.

Chatrou

Octopus in Guadeloupe and Martinique.

Chaudeau

A speciality from Guadeloupe, *chaudeau* is a mix of eggs, milk and spices, and is served at weddings, christenings and first communions. Its preparation is steeped in ritual: nothing else can be prepared in the same kitchen at the same time and the person preparing it cannot be on their time of the month. A good *chaudeau* is a sign of a successful party.

Chiquetaille

Shredded salted fish or meat marinated with herbs, onions, garlic, lime and chilli. See p.75.

Chocho (also known as chayote, chow chow, mirliton, christophine)

An edible plant, a gourd and a cousin of cucumber, originally from South America. Shaped like a pear and cream to light green in colour, its flesh is soft and watery and can be eaten raw but its core must be cooked. You can replace chocho with courgettes (zucchini) or cucumbers.

Colombo

A French Caribbean spice mix that gave its name to a curry dish made with chicken, pork, mutton, lamb, or even root vegetables. You can make your own (p.86) or replace it with regular curry powder.

Conch (known locally as *lambi*)

A mollusc that lives in a spiral-shaped seashell. Its very firm white flesh needs to be pounded to soften it before it is grilled, as the Amerindians did, or stewed in red sauce. Conch is now a protected species and it can be difficult to find.

Court bouillon

A cooking technique, primarily used to prepare red tropical fish. Creole court bouillon is a tomato-based broth in which the fish is poached. Not to be confused with the traditional French court bouillon. See p.110.

Dasheen (also known as taro, locally known as *madère* in Guadeloupe, *dachine* in Martinique)
A tuber with dark brown skin. This root has a white, sometimes purple-ish flesh and is usually boiled and both the root and its leaves can be eaten (*see* calalou).

Dutch pot, Dutch oven
Usually made of cast iron or aluminium, they have a well-fitting lid and distribute heat to the food very slowly and evenly perfect for Creole stews.

Féroce
A dish made from avocado, salted cod, cassava flour and quite a lot of hot chilli pepper, which makes it ferocious indeed. See pp.66 and 68.

Giraumon *see* calabaza

Ground provisions (also known as hard food)
The term covers vegetables such as yam, breadfruit, green bananas, plantains, cassava, dasheen (taro) and sweet potatoes. They are usually boiled and served as side dishes.

Guava
A pear-shaped fruit with a pink or white flesh that ripens from green to yellow. They are sweet and often used to make juice, punch, jam, jelly and a paste for baking. See p.225.

Malanga (eddo)
A tuber with dark brown skin; very similar to dasheen (taro) but smaller.

Matété (Guadeloupe) or Matoutou (Martinique)
A traditional rice dish made with blue land crab, usually eaten on Easter Monday. See p.120.

Migan
A very easy to make dish, typical of the French islands. Its traditional base is breadfruit and pumpkin with pork meats. See p.133.

Okra (also known as ladies' fingers, locally known as gombo)
A green pod with white edible seeds, it forms the base of many African and Caribbean stews.

Ouassou (Guadeloupe), z'habitant (Martinique)
A variety of prawn (shrimp) local to the Caribbean islands. It lives in fresh water close to the source of rivers and can be compared to crayfish. It is also called giant river prawn, giant freshwater prawn, Malaysian prawn, freshwater scampi or Rosenberg prawn.

Pain au beurre et chocolat
A Martinique classic that literally means 'butter bread and chocolate'. The *pain au beurre* is a plaited brioche that takes hours and real flair to make. It is served with hot chocolate made with pure cocoa.

Pâté en pot
A Martinique institution: a very thick soup made with offal, vegetables and capers, it's made for all types of celebrations. See p.176.

Plantain
It's a banana, but not a fruit, a vegetable, always cooked before eating. It starts off green and hard and ripens to yellow, and then goes black.

Rhum agricole
This literally means 'agricultural rum', as opposed to industrially produced rum. Rhum agricole is distilled from freshly squeezed sugar cane juice rather than molasses. It is produced in Guadeloupe, Martinique and Haiti.

Saltfish

Saltfish is fish that is salt-cured and dried. In the Caribbean it is almost universally understood to mean salted cod. It could be any fish, although it does tend to be white fish such as cod or pollock. But herring, shark and snapper, among others, can also be saltfish.

Shrubb

A liqueur made from rum infused with orange peel and sugar, traditionally drunk at Christmas. Why is it spelt with two b's? I'm not sure why, but that's Creole! See p.52.

Sorrel (also known as roselle or hibiscus, locally known as *groseille pays*)

The flower of the *Hibiscus sabdariffa* comes from West Africa, where it's called *bissap*, and is used to make syrup, jelly and punch, especially during the Christmas season in the Caribbean. Dried sorrel is available all year round in Afro-Caribbean shops and fresh sorrel can be found in the month or two leading up to Christmas in these same shops. It is also sold, as hibiscus flowers, in Turkish and Persian shops.

Souskay

A dish named after the preparation technique, which entails soaking fruits in a savoury vinaigrette of lime, garlic, salt and chilli. See p.84.

Yam

A very large tuber with thick, rough, dark brown skin. The starchy flesh can be either white or yellow, the yellow-fleshed variety being the most widely available in the Caribbean.

WHERE TO SHOP

UK ONLINE

Afro Caribbean Store – afrocaribbeanstore.co.uk

My Afro Foodstore – myafrofoodstore.com

The Asian Cookshop – theasiancookshop.co.uk

Avila UK – avilauk.com

Blue Mountain Peak – bluemountainpeak.com

Carib Gourmet – carib-gourmet.com

Caribbean Supermarket
caribbeansupermarket.co.uk

The Fish Society – thefishsociety.co.uk

Grace Foods UK/Caribbean Food Centre
caribbeanfoodcentre.com

Lisboa – lisboaloja.co.uk

Longdan – longdan.co.uk

See Woo – seewoouk.com

Tropical Sun Foods – tropicalsunfoods.com

Vincy Foods/Caribbean Trade UK Ltd
vincyfoods.co.uk

USA ONLINE

First World Imports – firstworldimports.com

Grace Foods – buygracefoods.com

Sam's Caribbean Online Store – sams247.com

West Indian Shop – westindianshop.com

INDEX

ACKNOWLEDGEMENTS

I would like to thank you for buying this book and deciding to make some room for Creole food in your kitchen.

I would like to thank my agent Elise Dillsworth and my editor Emily Preece-Morrison. Big shout-out to Rosie, Ellie, Clare, Wei and the whole team that guided me through completing this dream of mine.

I would like to thank my family. My father – just mentioning your name or talking about you still brings me to tears. You always believed I'd write a book: you probably thought it would be Creole Caribbean literature, fiction or poetry, as that's what you used to correct for me. I remember getting angry with you, since I thought your comments were too harsh. I wish you'd read over this book. I love you. Thank you for making me the cook I am today. My mother, who covers me with love and support – since my father died, she gives enough love for both. She is the strongest, most generous, sensitive and loving parent one could wish for. She's an ace cook, too, and I respect her so much. My brother Sébastien and my sister Cindy. We are a clan; can't wait to cook (and argue like we always do) again in the kitchen.

I would like to thank Pierre Antoine, the love of my life.

I would like to thank my friends Audrey and Daniela, who are like sisters to me, and Samantha, Jessica and Thaïna for testing the recipes one way or another. I'd like to thank Jenny, Sally and my group of Frenchies for encouraging me. All the students I've taught over the past few years, who have made me a better cook, as well as the customers who have come to my supper club. And above all I'd like to thank God, because my faith is also part of my culture and I believe He masters everything!